AF261444

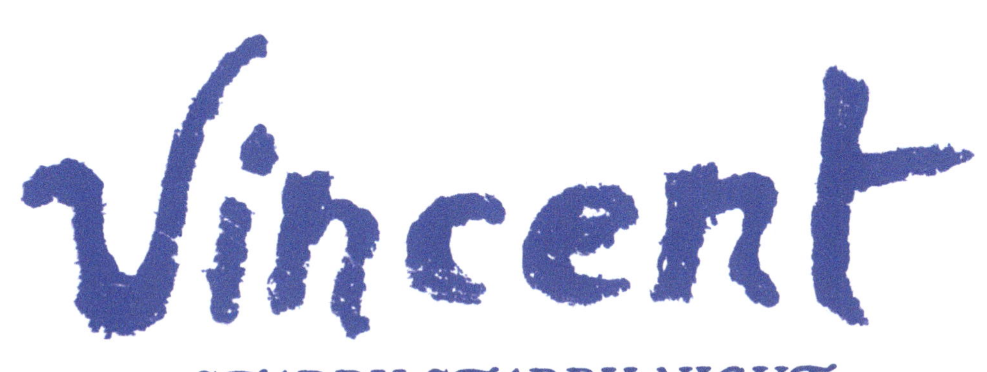

STARRY STARRY NIGHT

WRITTEN *by* JUDITH A. PROFFER

INRODUCTION *by* DON McLEAN

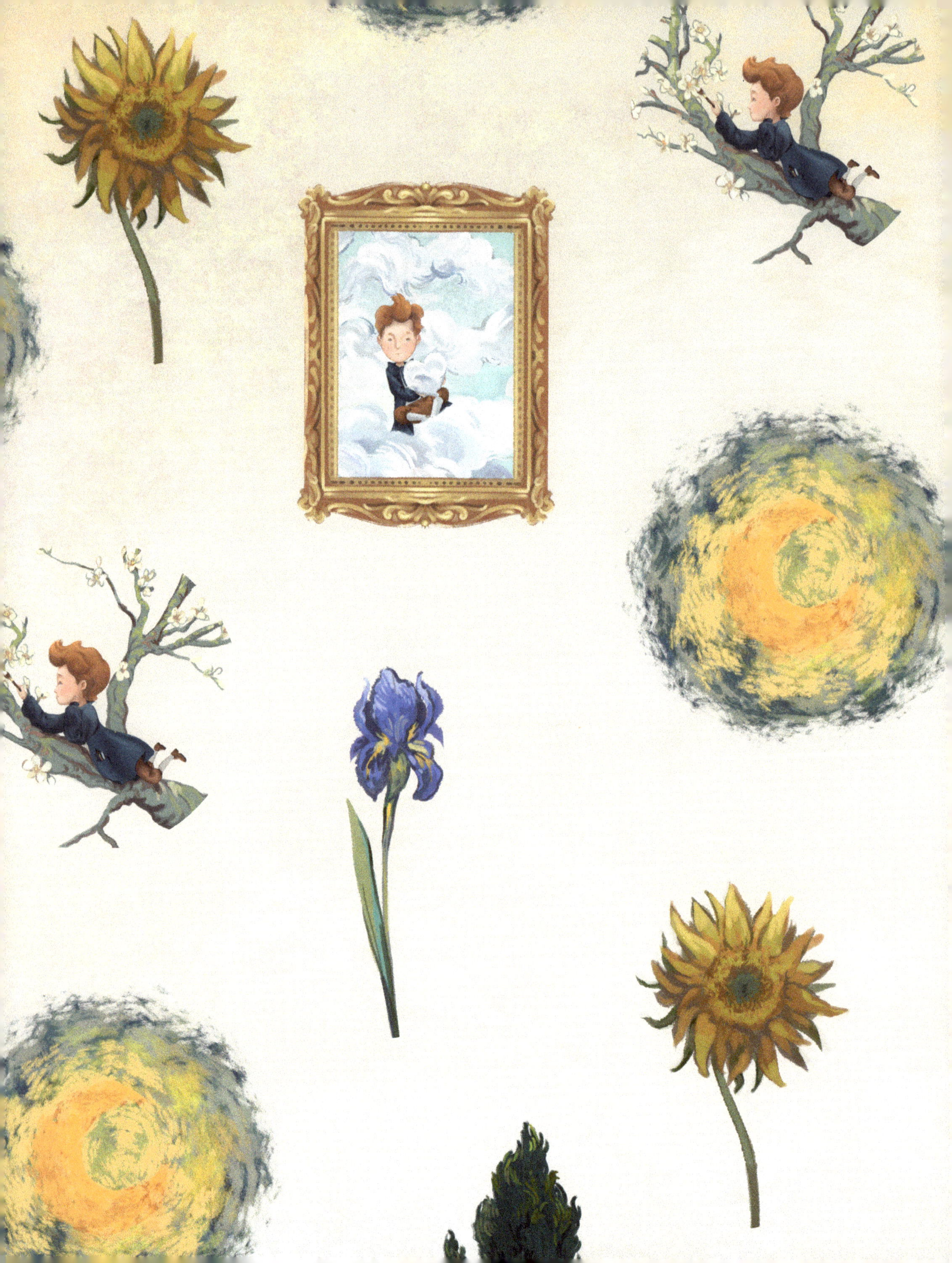

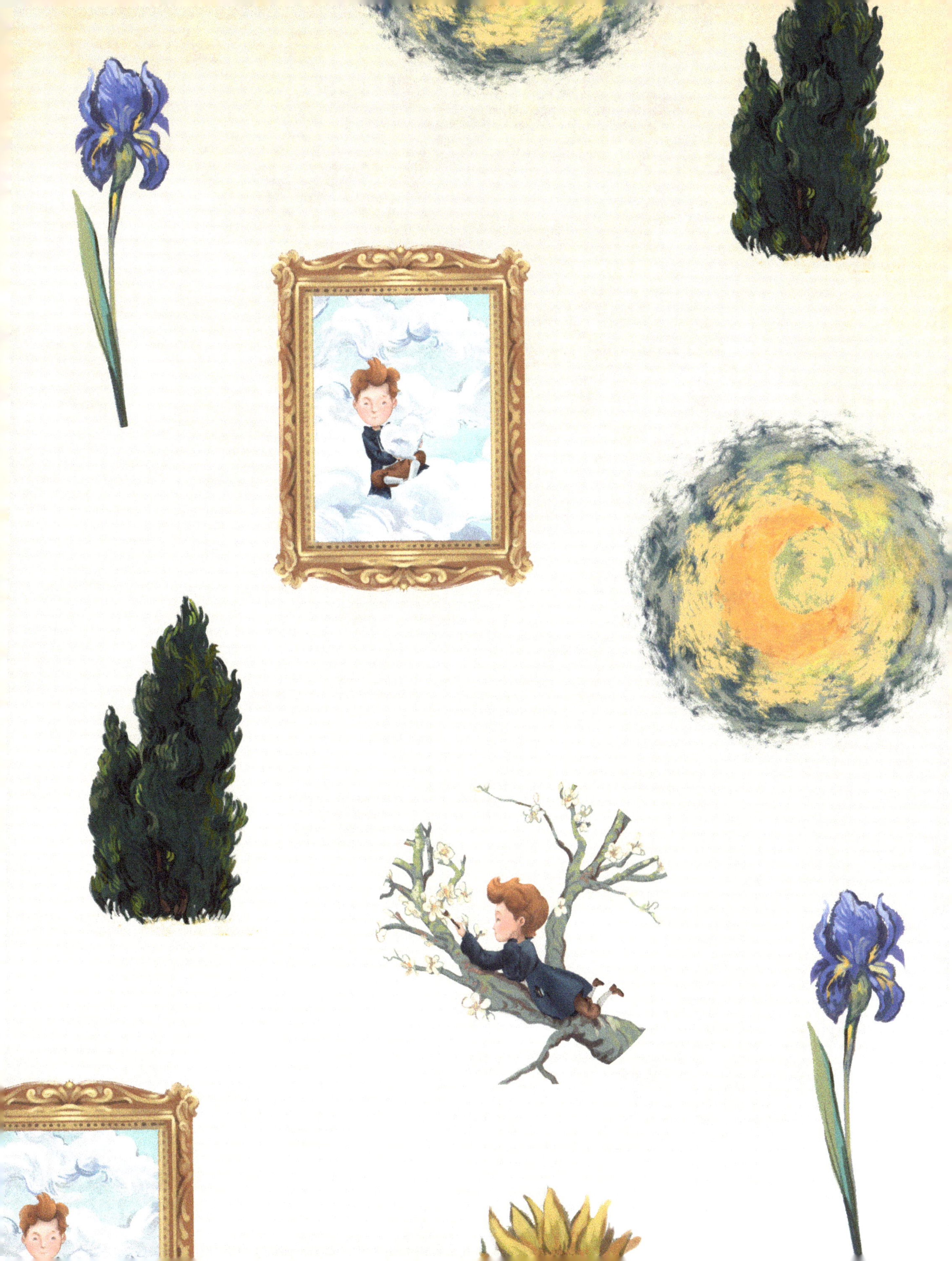

Vincent: Starry Starry Night

Judith A. Proffer

Copyright 2024: Morling Manor Music Corporation
All rights reserved

Cover and interior art by Yoko Matsuoka

Art direction by Judith A. Proffer

Cover and interior design by designSimple

Don McLean Management Representation:
Kirt Webster, Spinning Plates, Inc.

ISBN 978-1-7353844-5-0
Printed in the United States of America

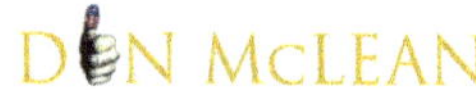

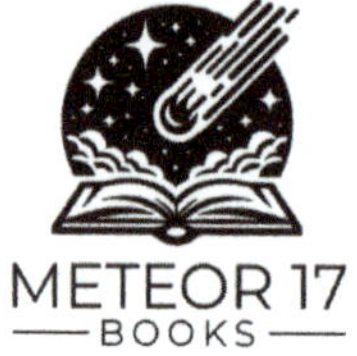

www.meteor17.com

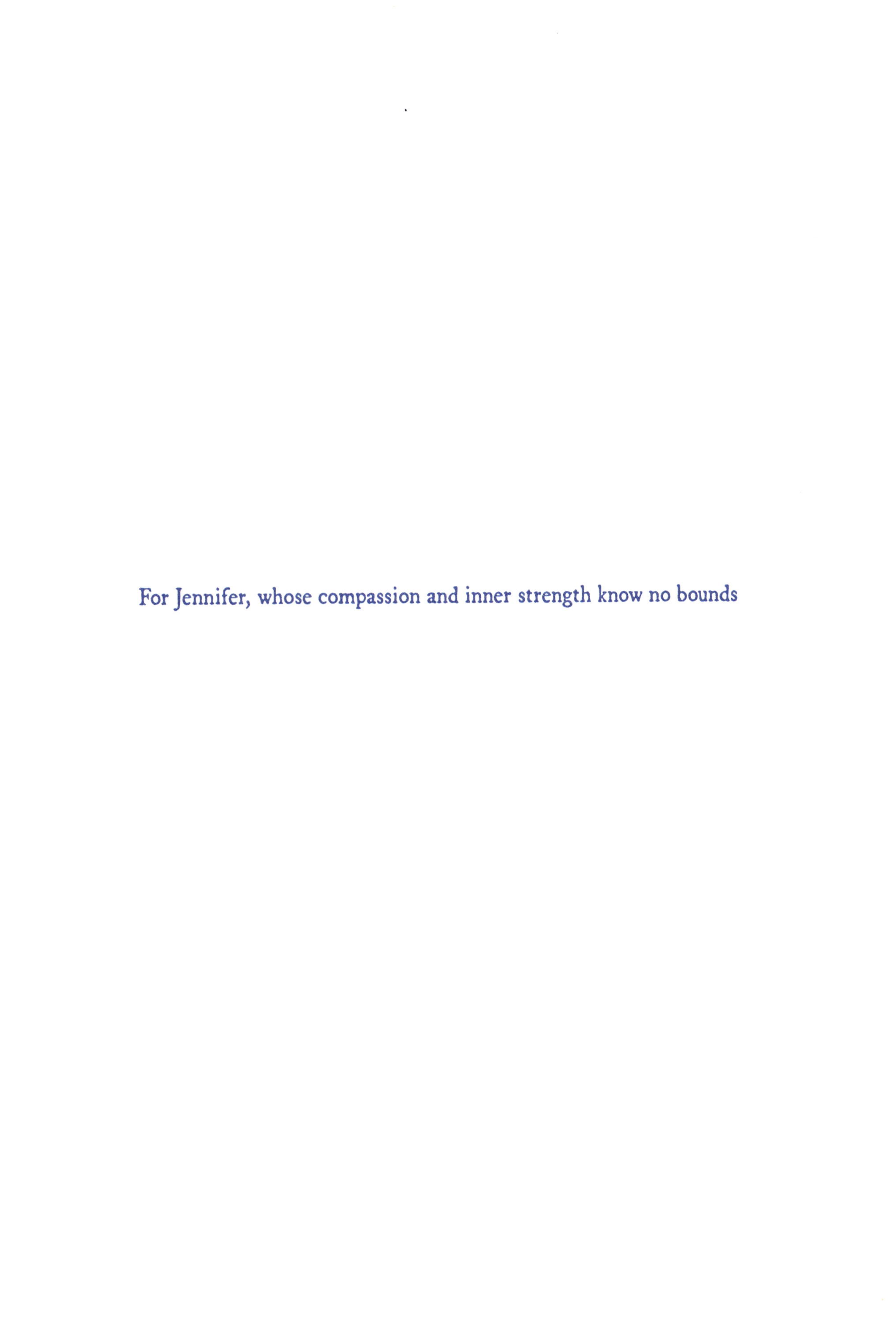

For Jennifer, whose compassion and inner strength know no bounds

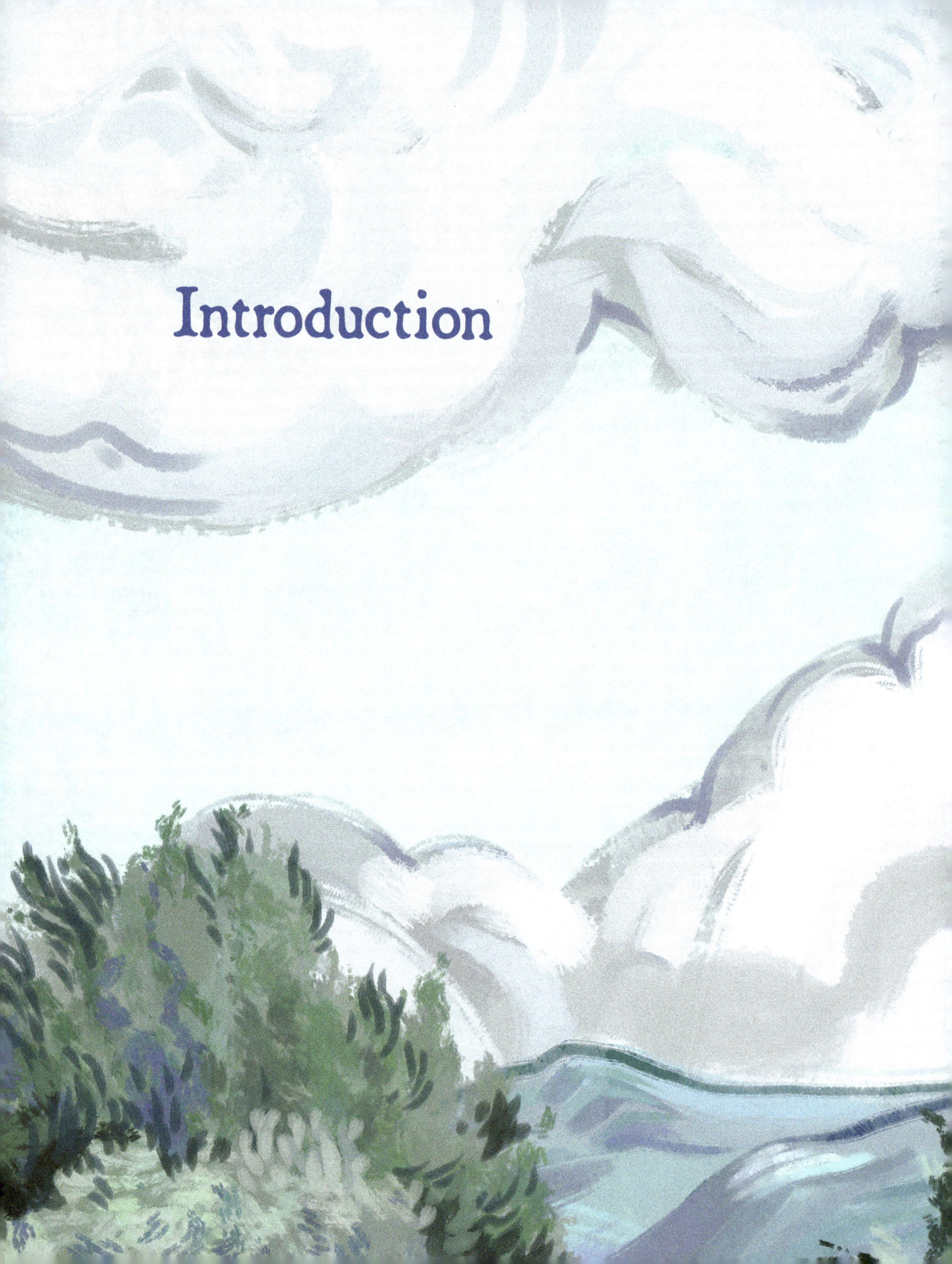

Introduction

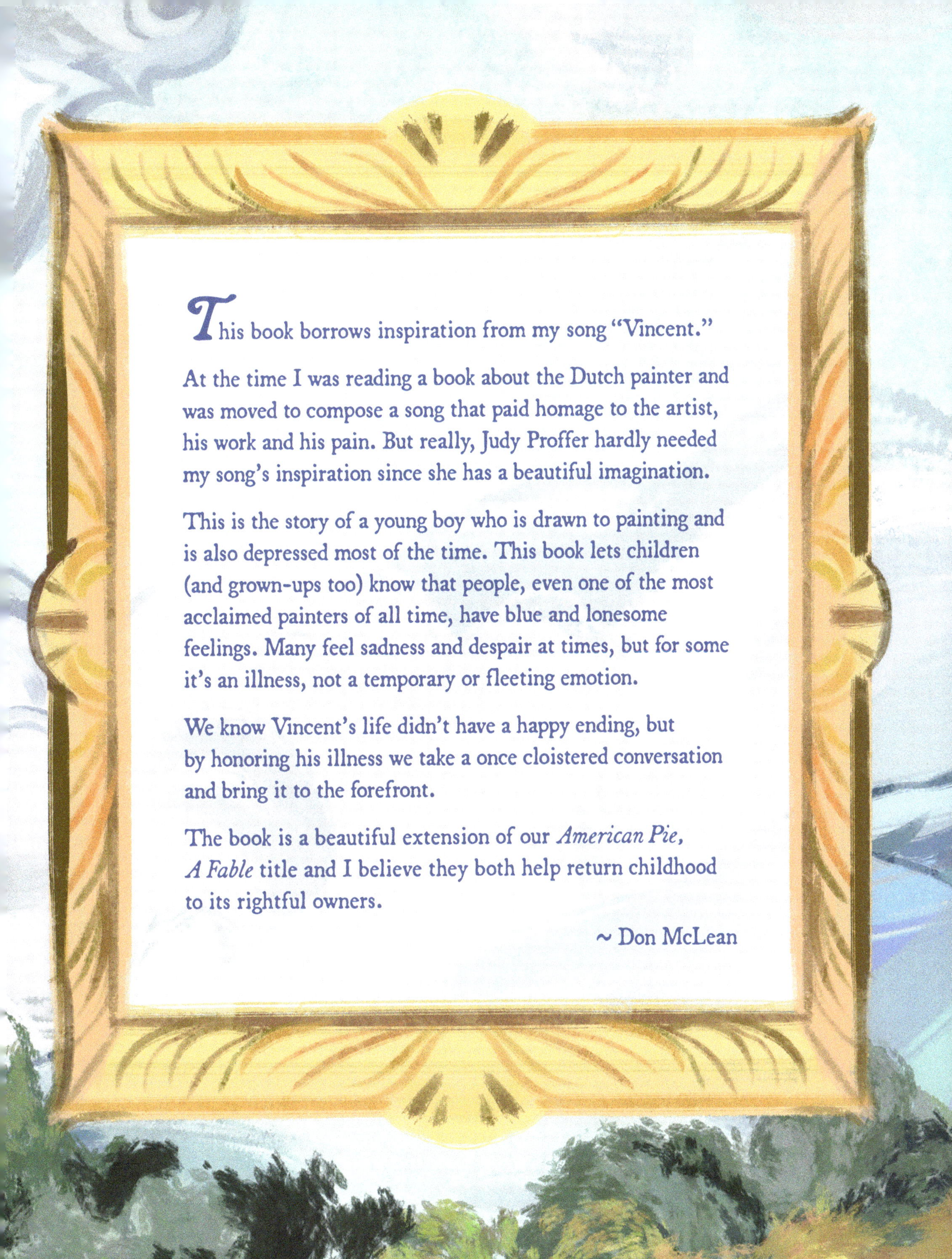

This book borrows inspiration from my song "Vincent."

At the time I was reading a book about the Dutch painter and was moved to compose a song that paid homage to the artist, his work and his pain. But really, Judy Proffer hardly needed my song's inspiration since she has a beautiful imagination.

This is the story of a young boy who is drawn to painting and is also depressed most of the time. This book lets children (and grown-ups too) know that people, even one of the most acclaimed painters of all time, have blue and lonesome feelings. Many feel sadness and despair at times, but for some it's an illness, not a temporary or fleeting emotion.

We know Vincent's life didn't have a happy ending, but by honoring his illness we take a once cloistered conversation and bring it to the forefront.

The book is a beautiful extension of our American Pie, A Fable title and I believe they both help return childhood to its rightful owners.

~ Don McLean

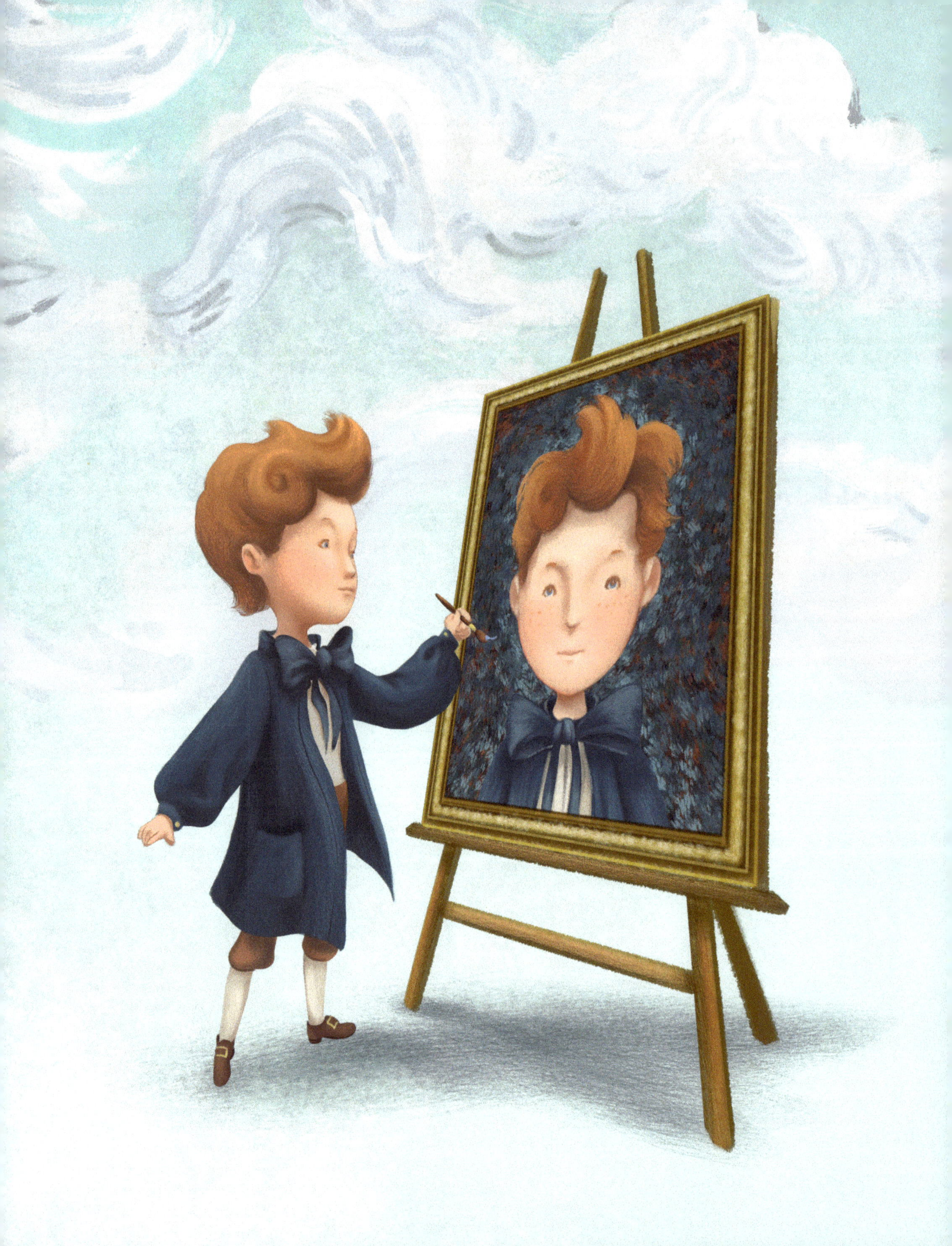

A long, long time ago lived a shy and fairly quiet boy named Vincent.

Vincent's busy hair blazed a fiery copper color. His eyes were the blue of the bluest irises in an early spring garden.

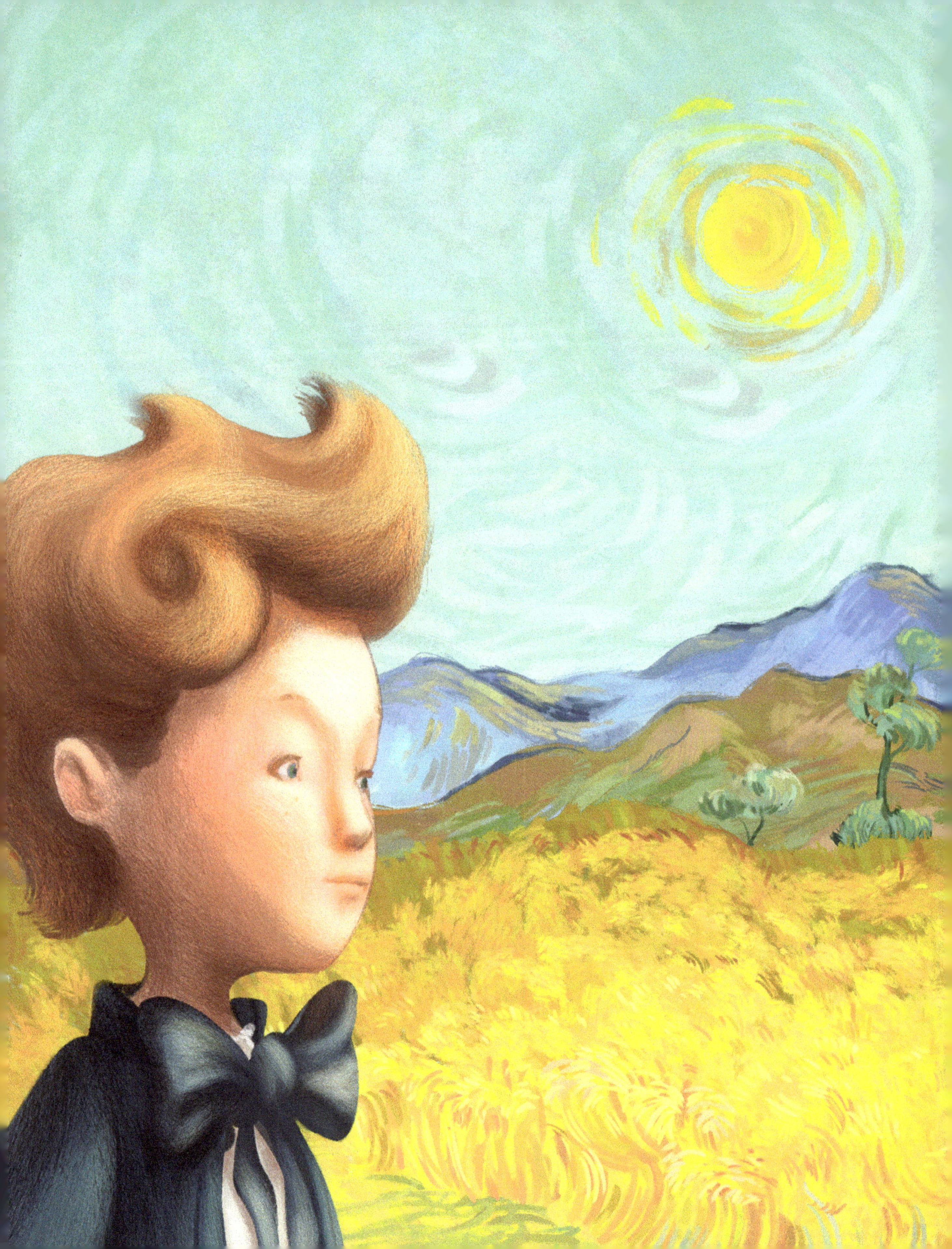

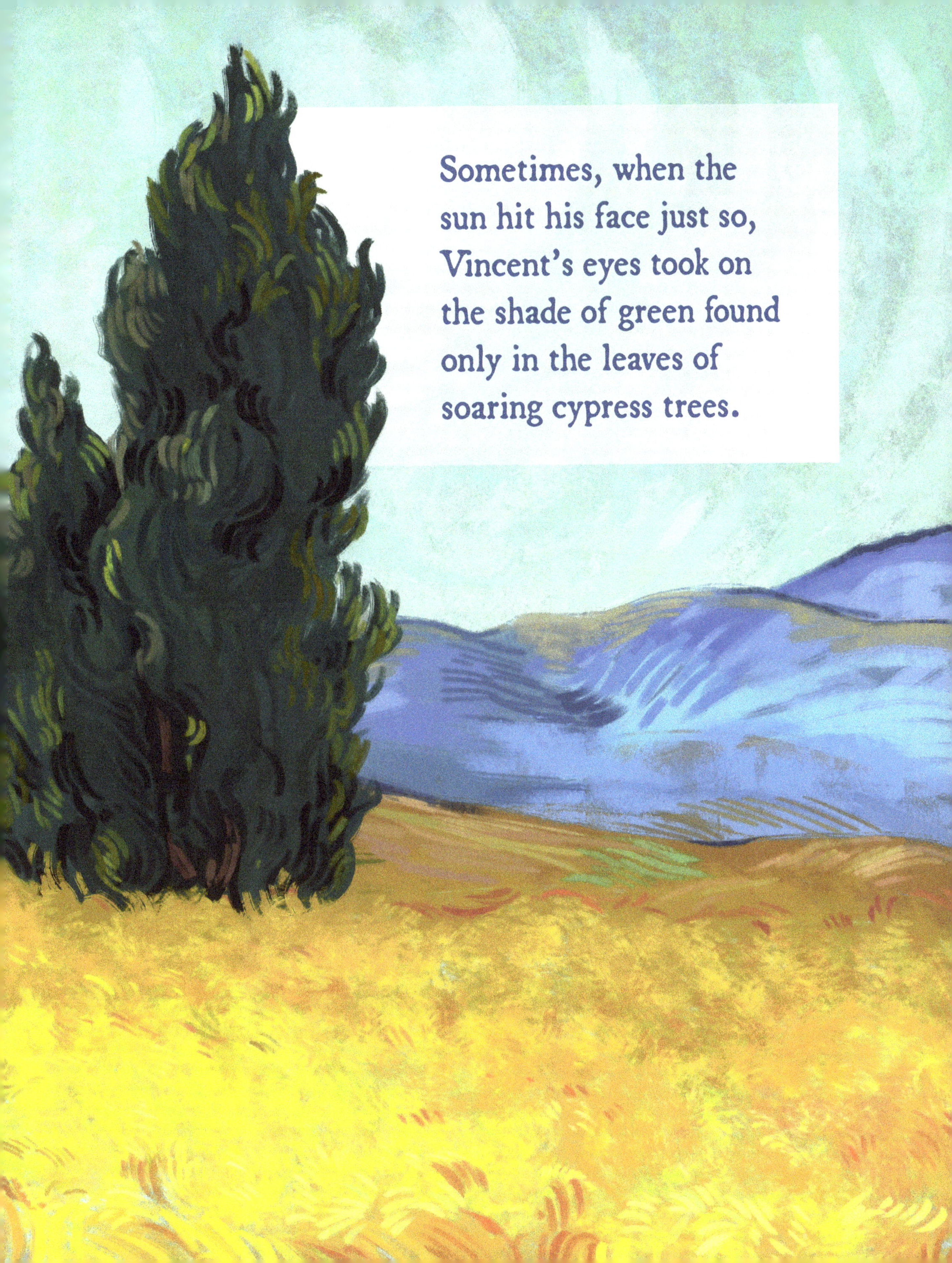
Sometimes, when the
sun hit his face just so,
Vincent's eyes took on
the shade of green found
only in the leaves of
soaring cypress trees.

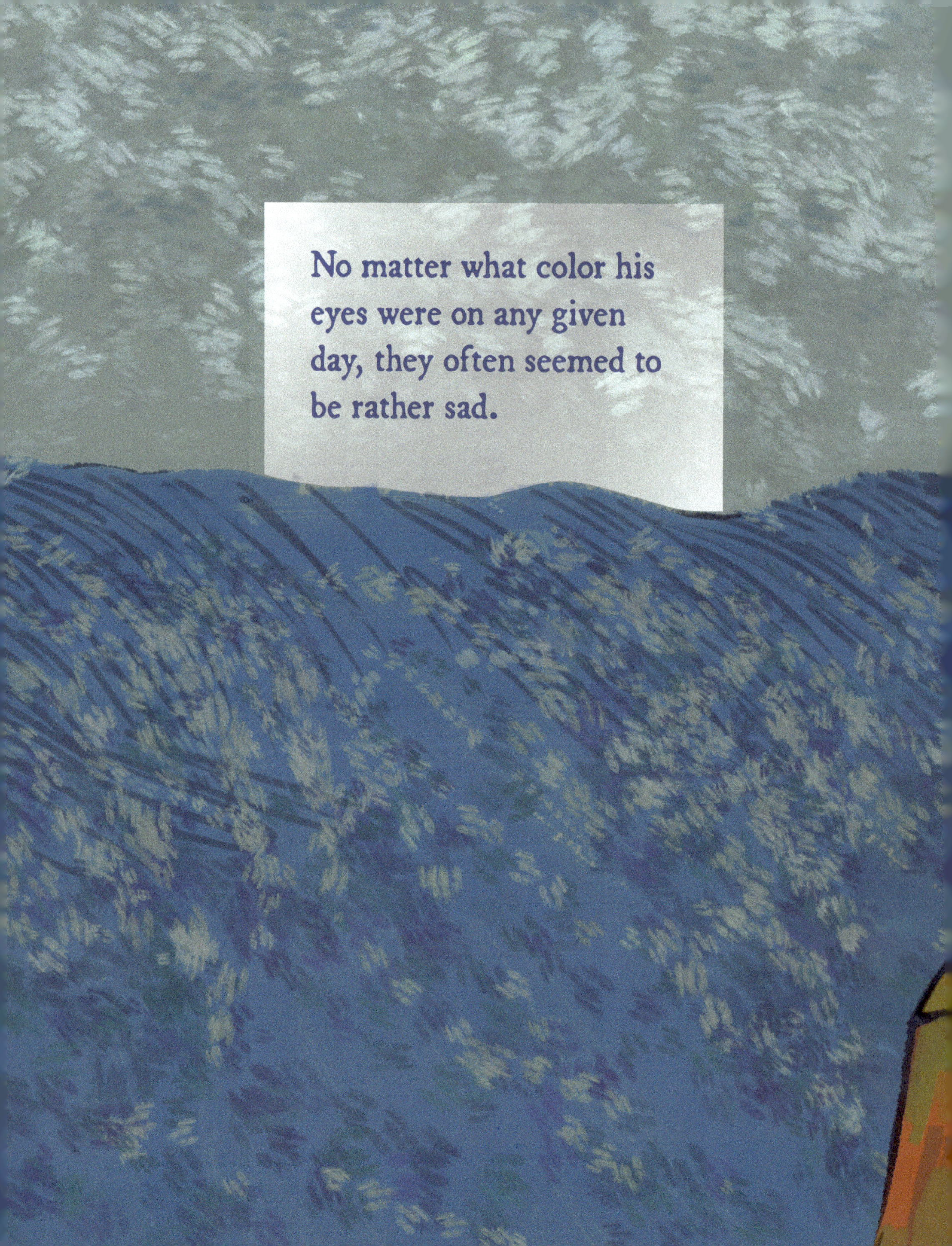
No matter what color his
eyes were on any given
day, they often seemed to
be rather sad.

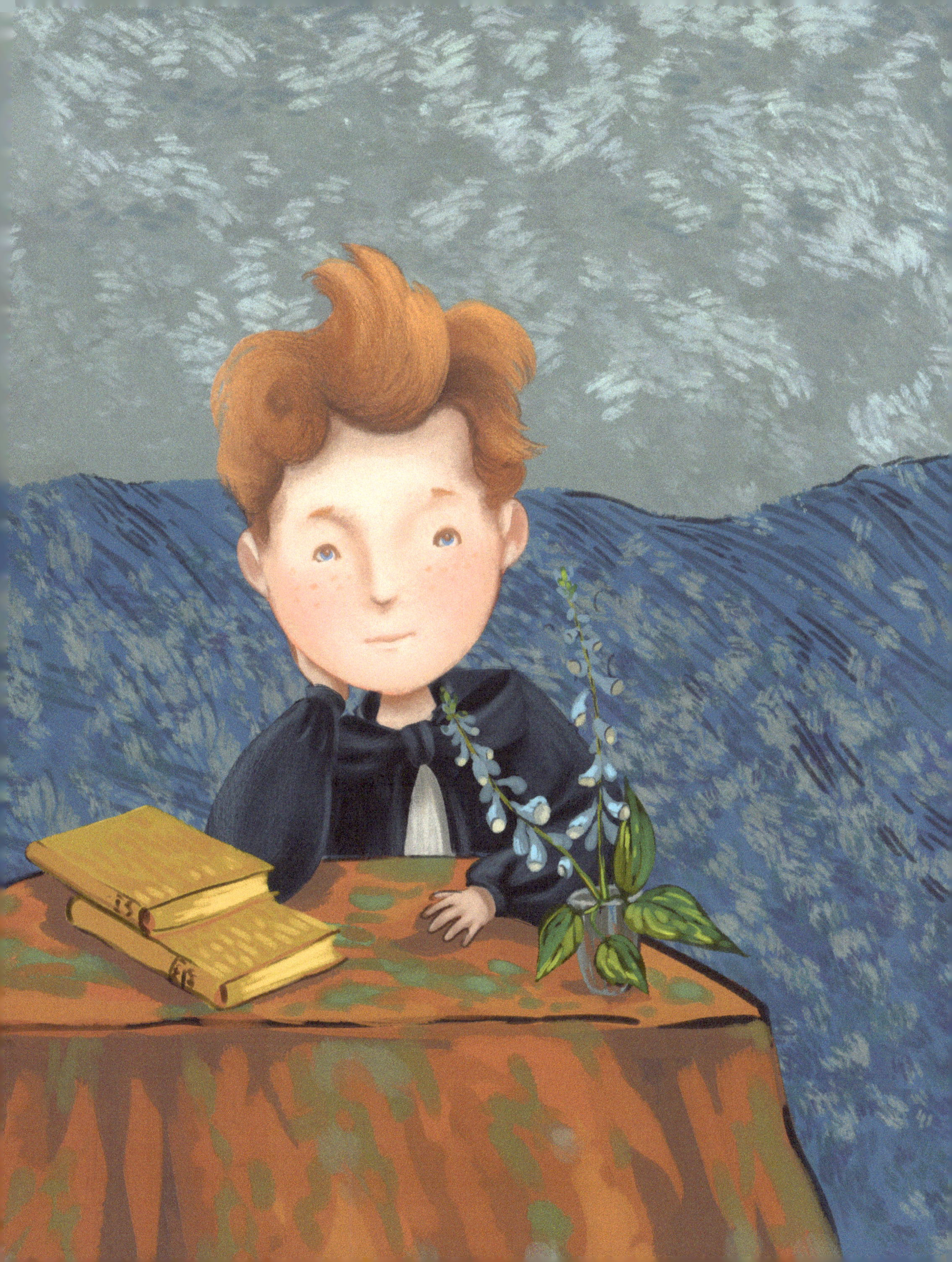

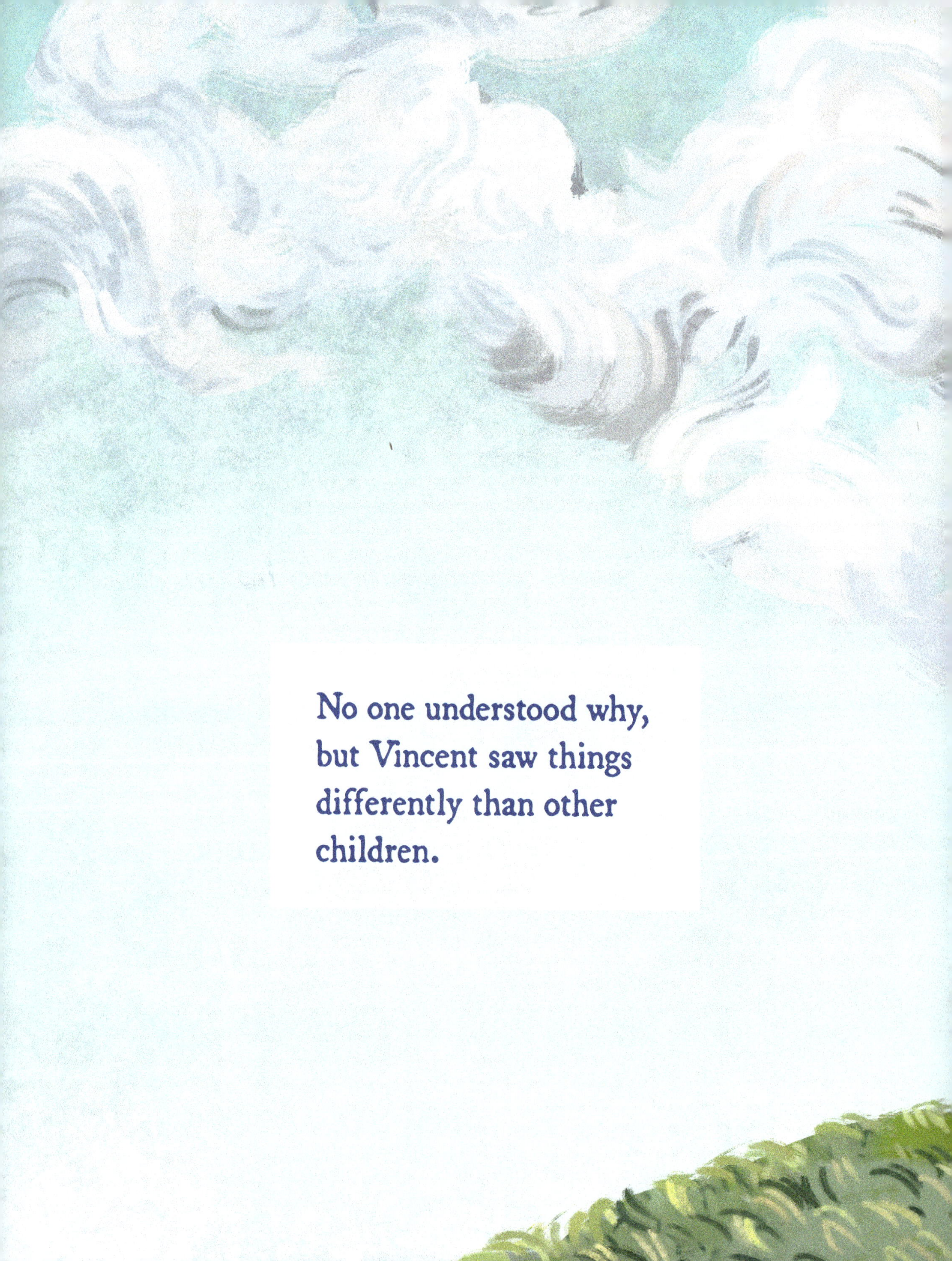

No one understood why,
but Vincent saw things
differently than other
children.

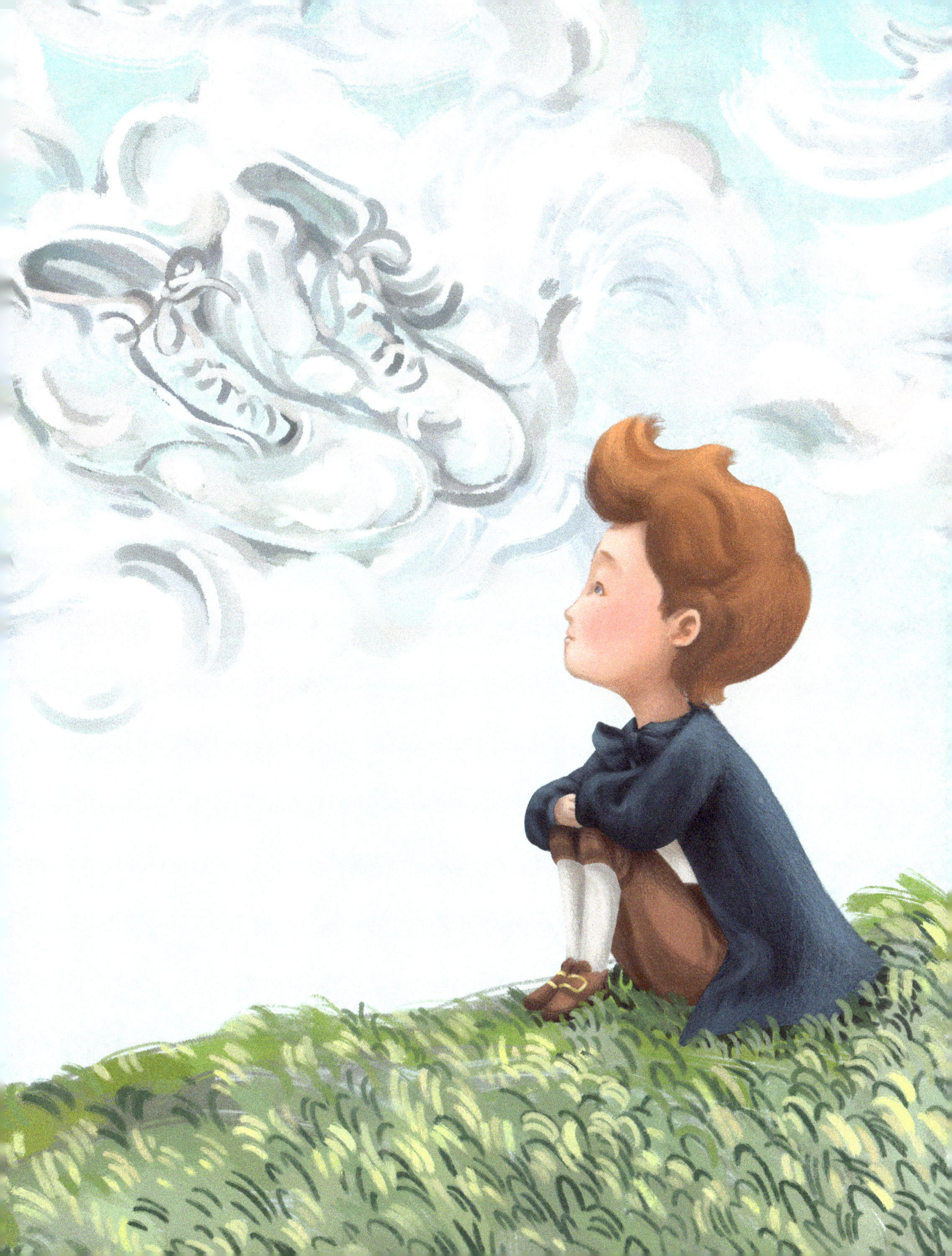

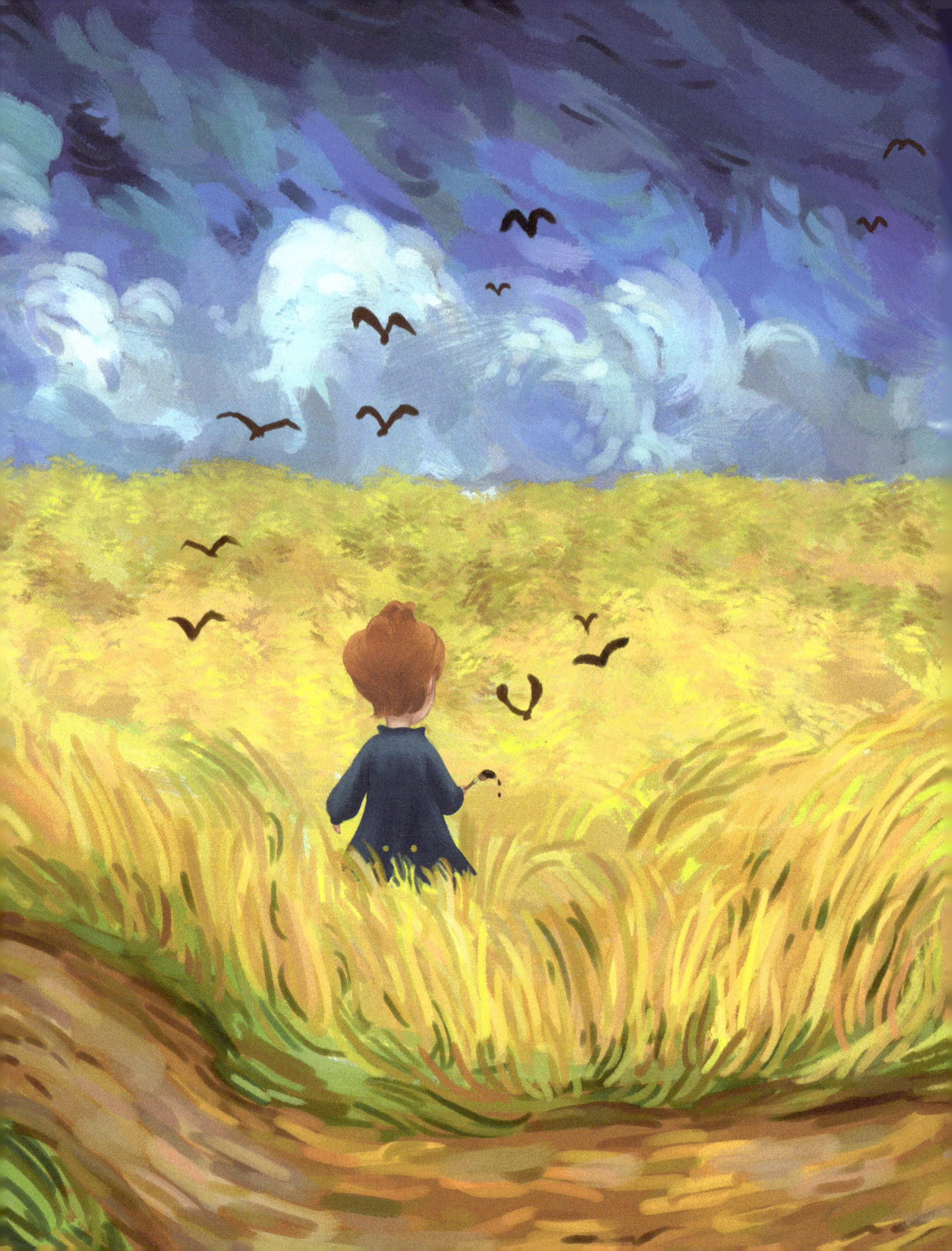

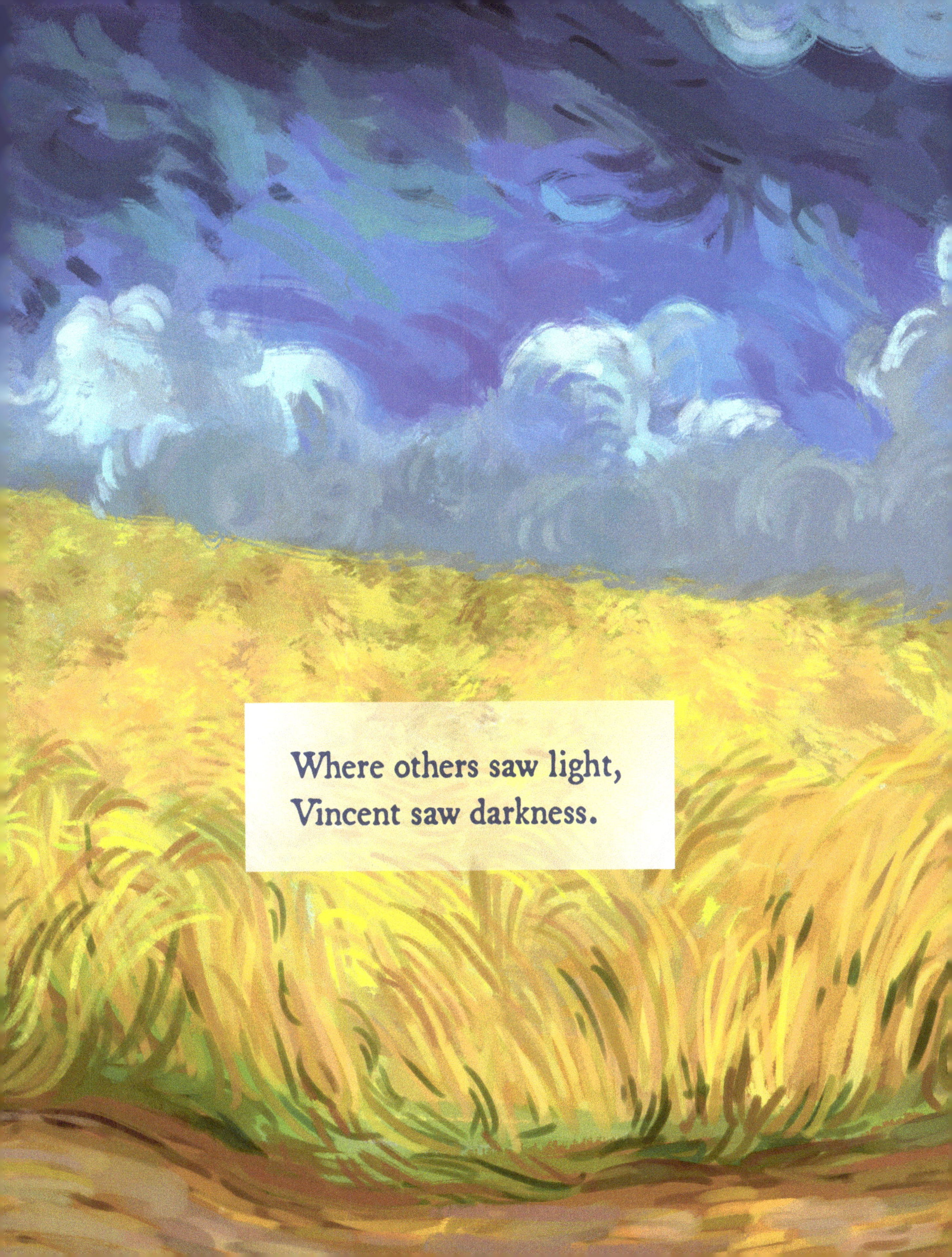
Where others saw light,
Vincent saw darkness.

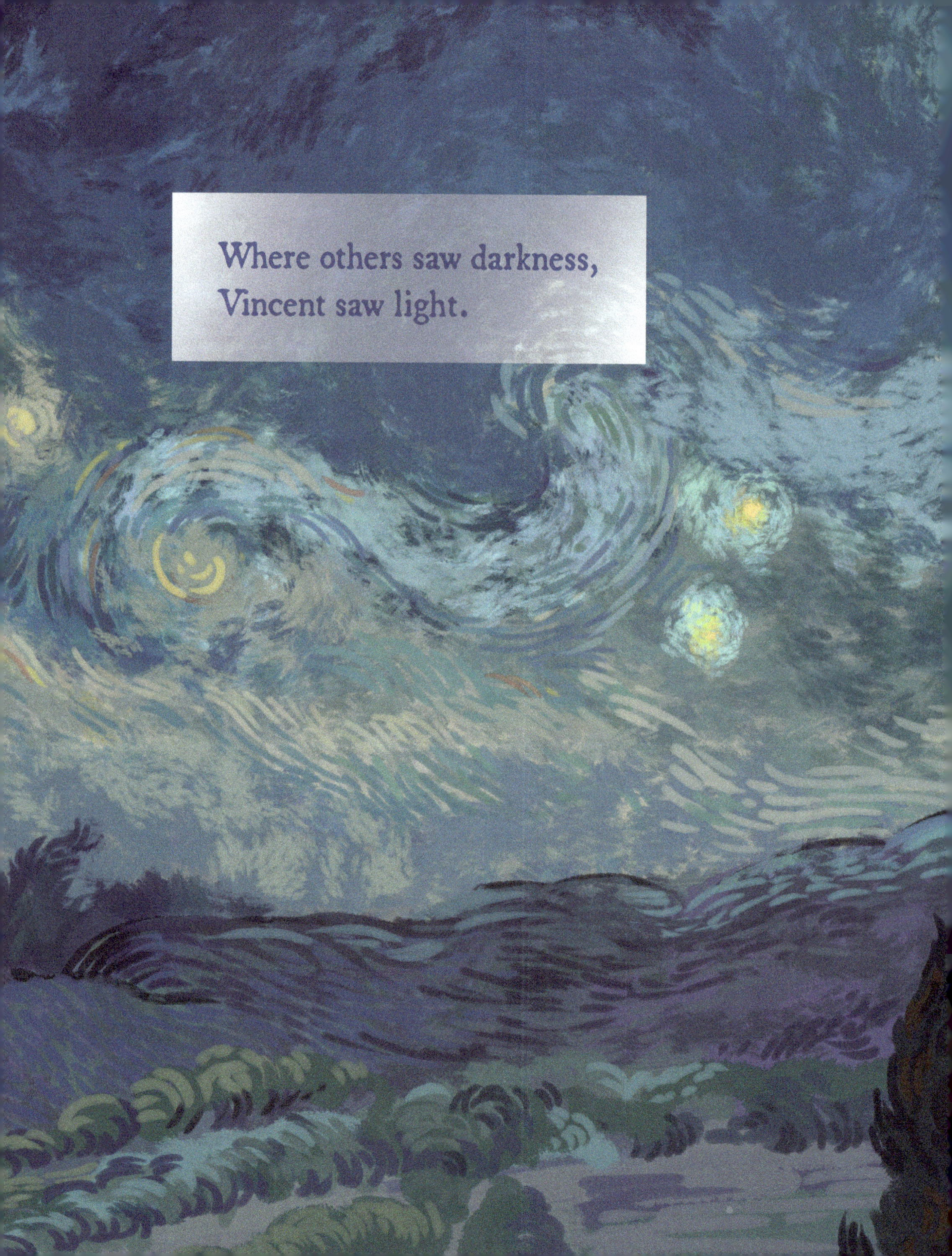

Where others saw darkness,
Vincent saw light.

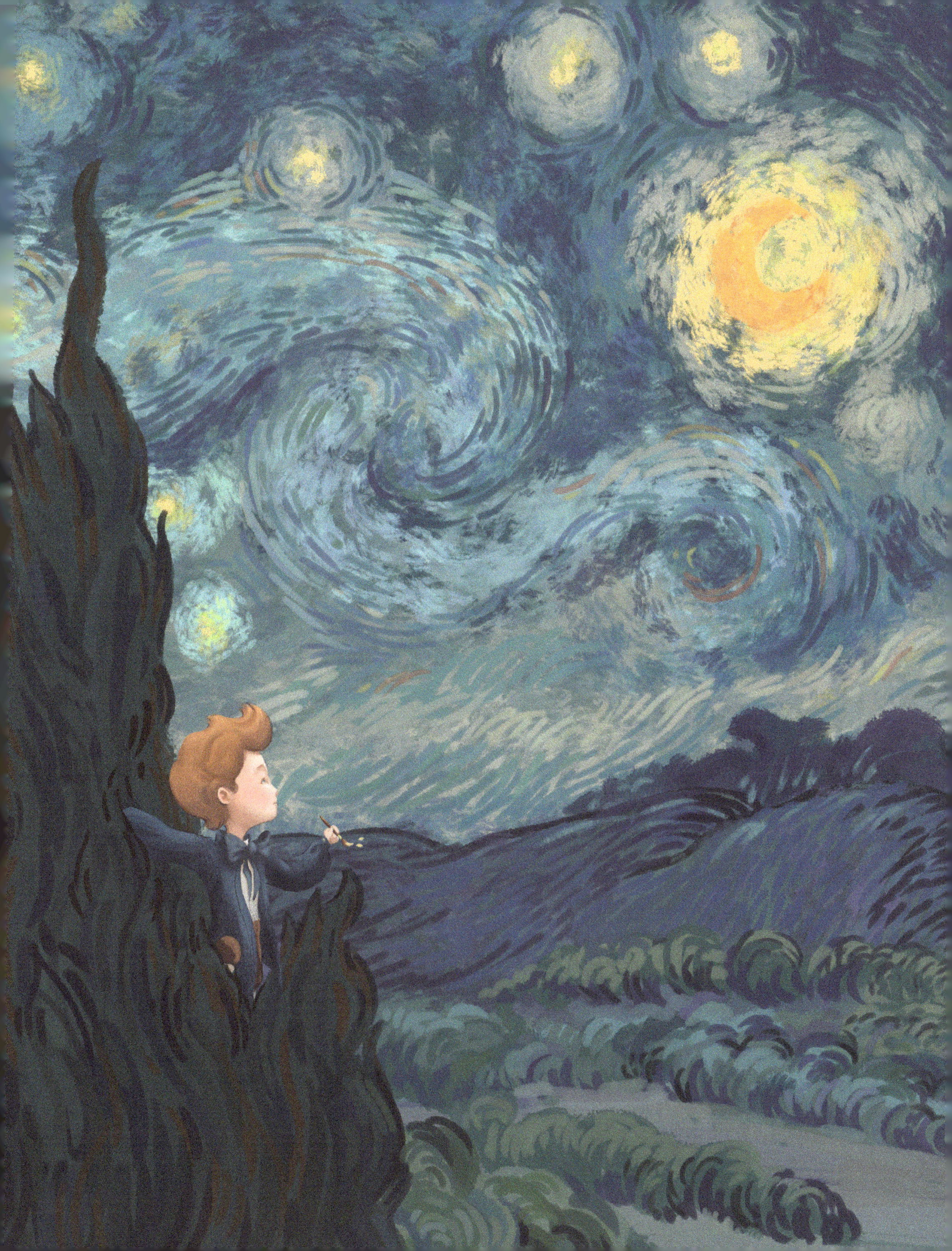

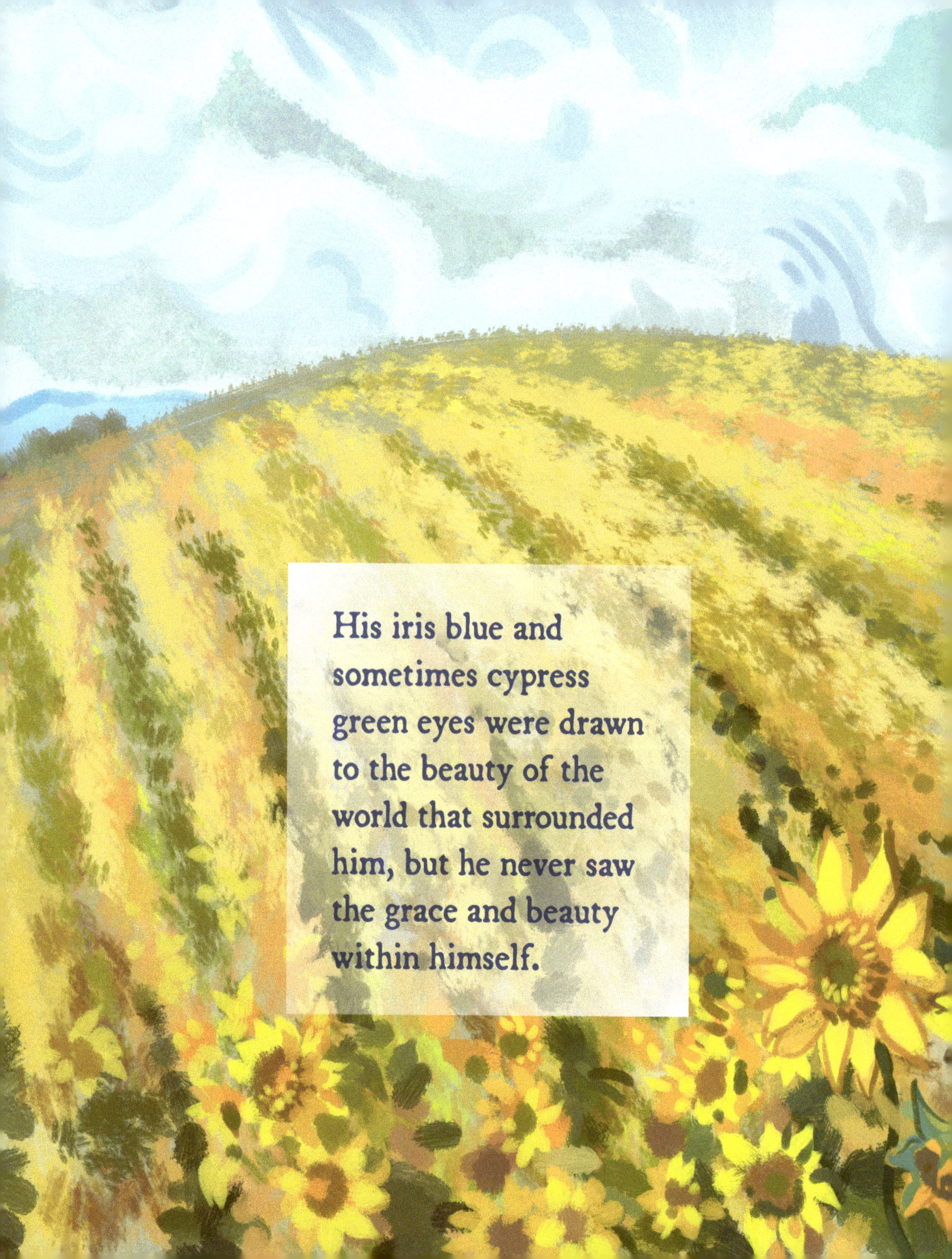
His iris blue and
sometimes cypress
green eyes were drawn
to the beauty of the
world that surrounded
him, but he never saw
the grace and beauty
within himself.

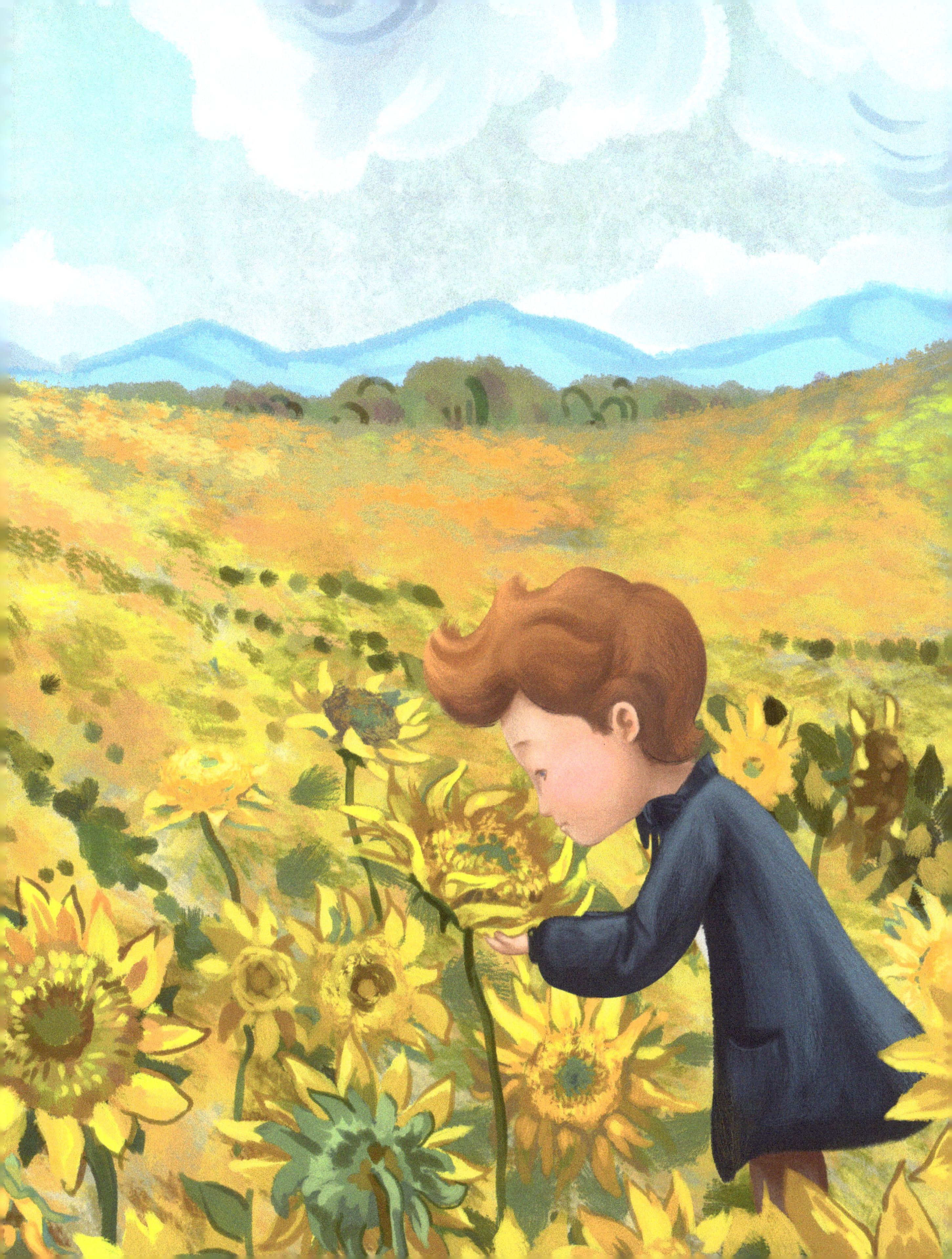

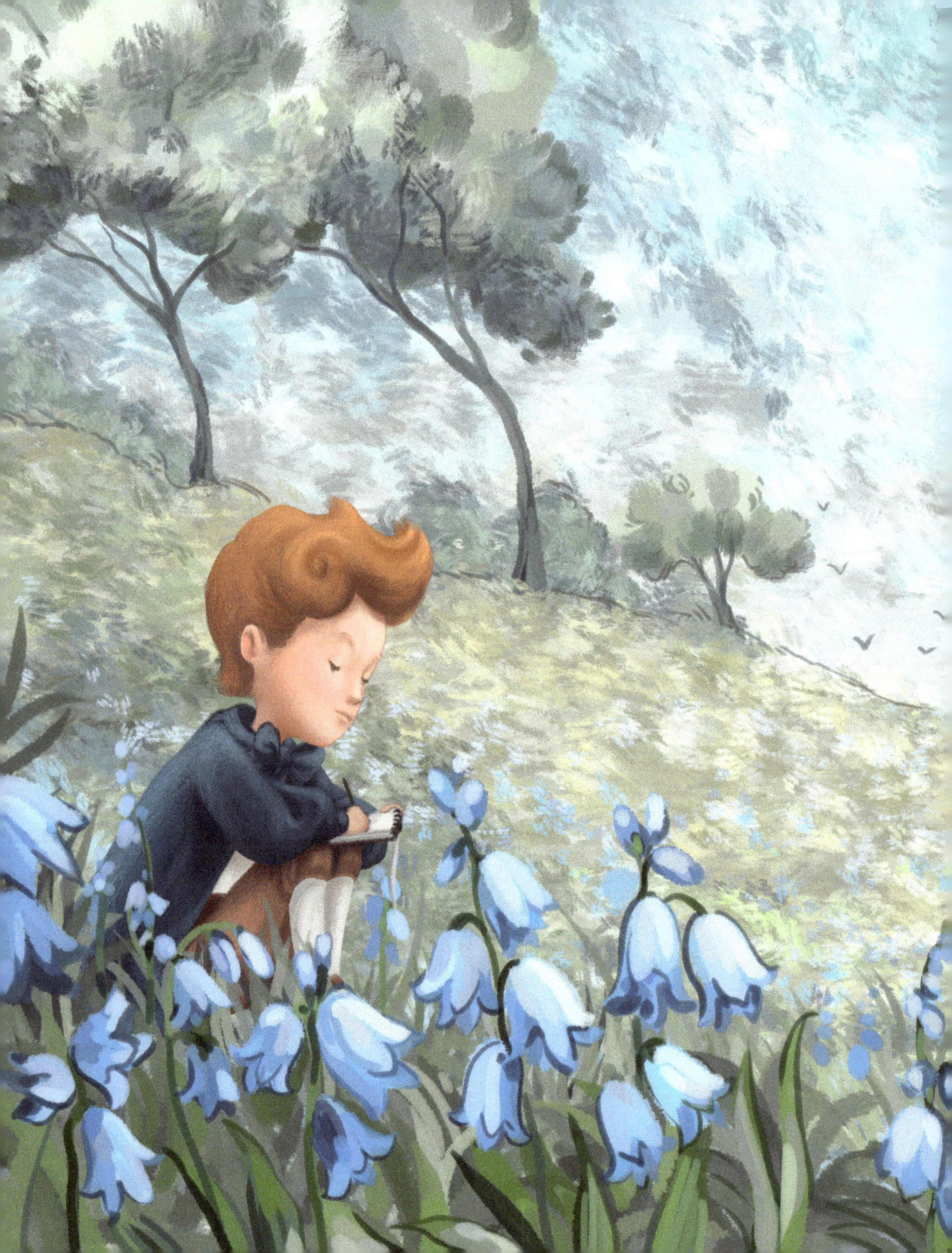

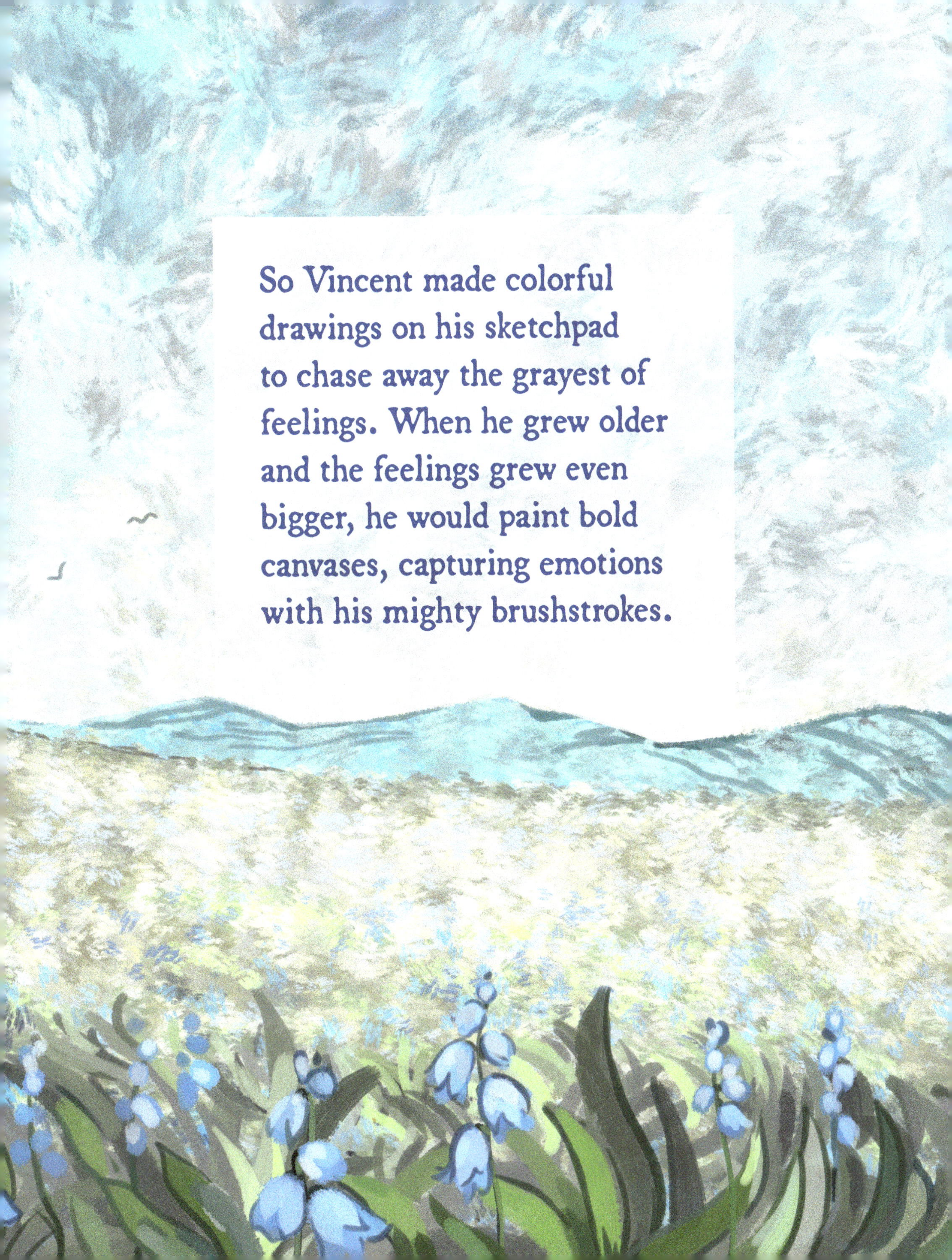

So Vincent made colorful
drawings on his sketchpad
to chase away the grayest of
feelings. When he grew older
and the feelings grew even
bigger, he would paint bold
canvases, capturing emotions
with his mighty brushstrokes.

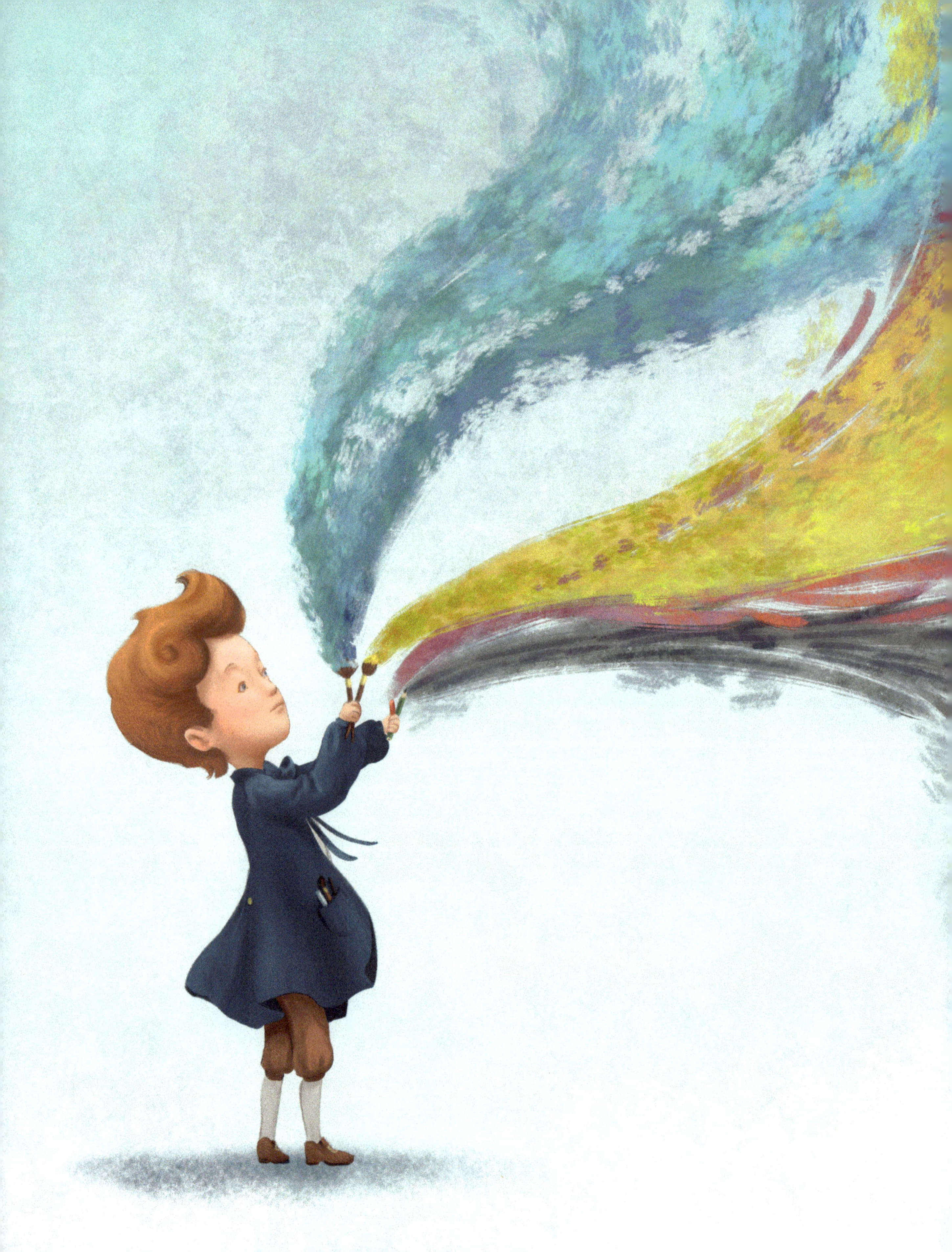

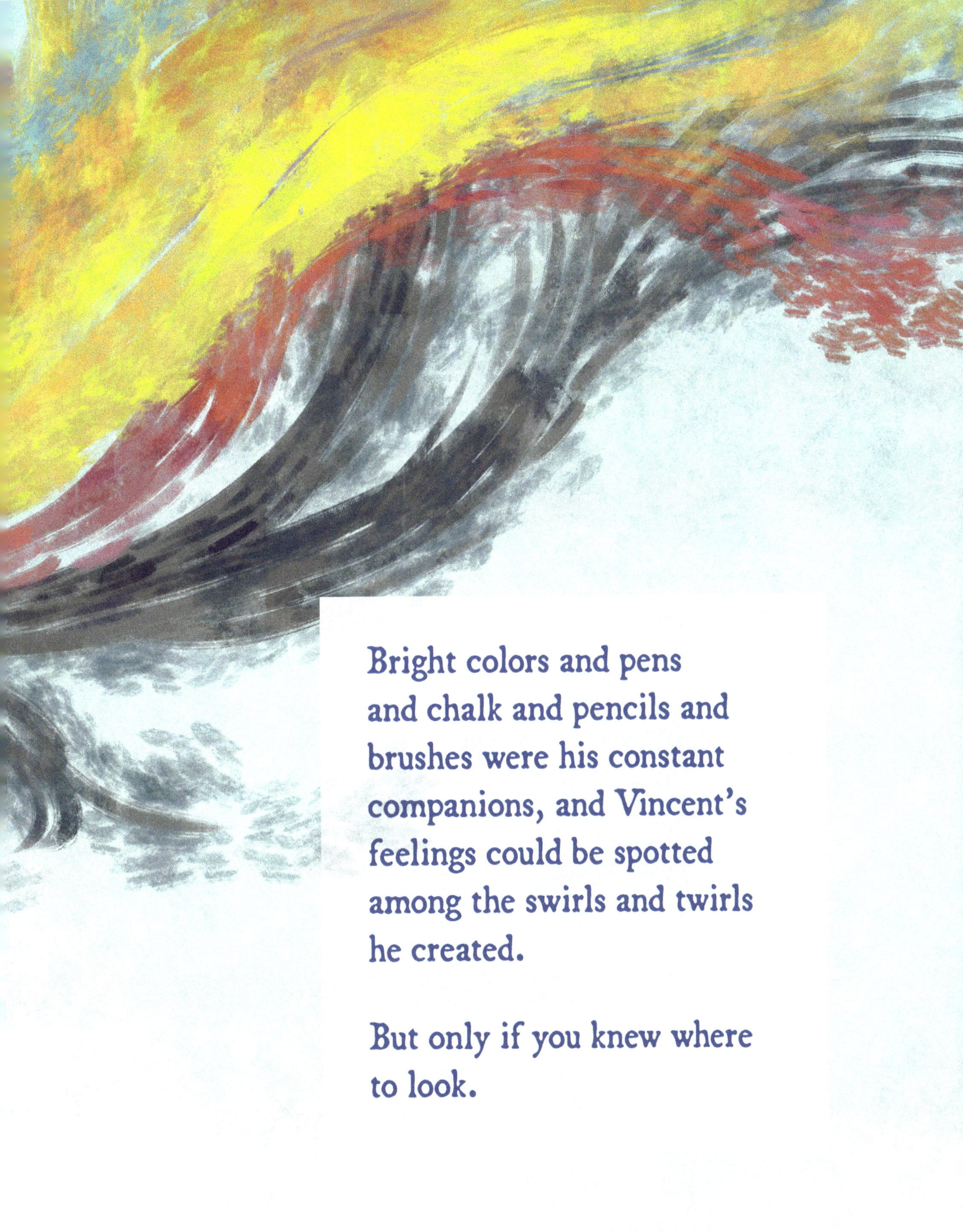

Bright colors and pens
and chalk and pencils and
brushes were his constant
companions, and Vincent's
feelings could be spotted
among the swirls and twirls
he created.

But only if you knew where
to look.

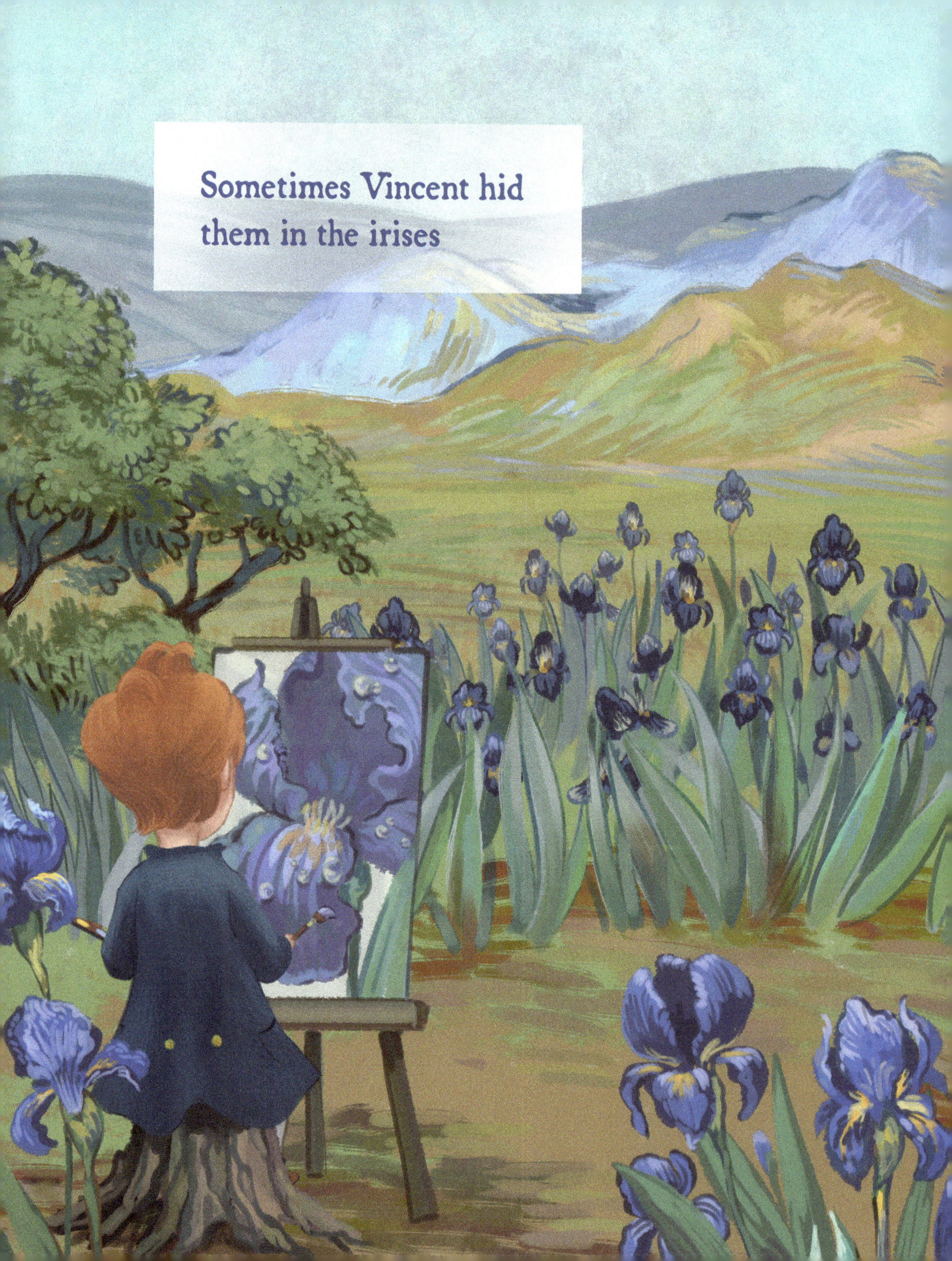
Sometimes Vincent hid
them in the irises

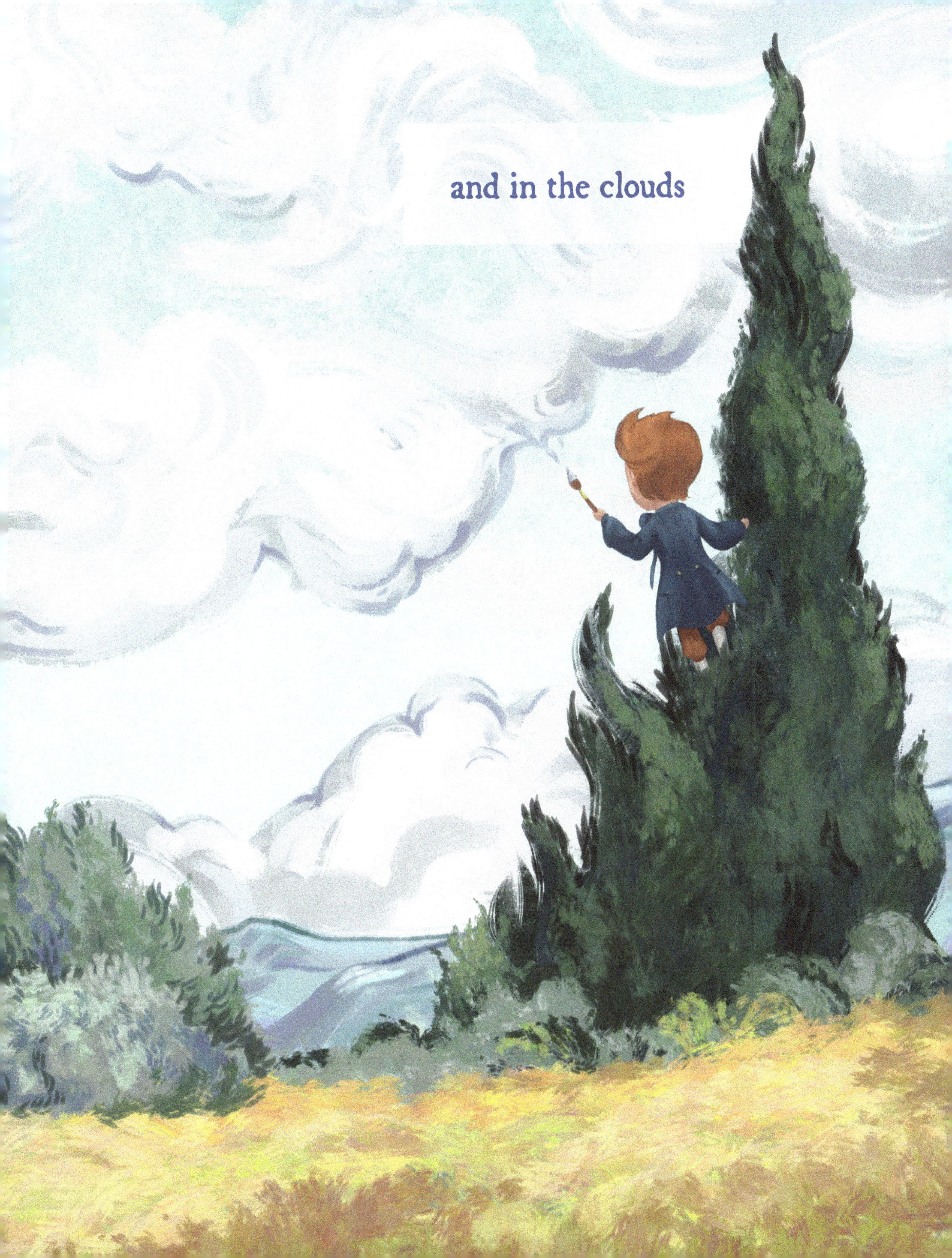
and in the clouds

and among the almond trees too.

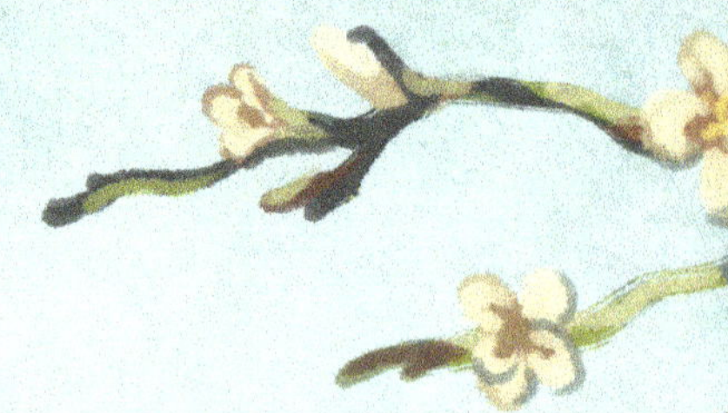

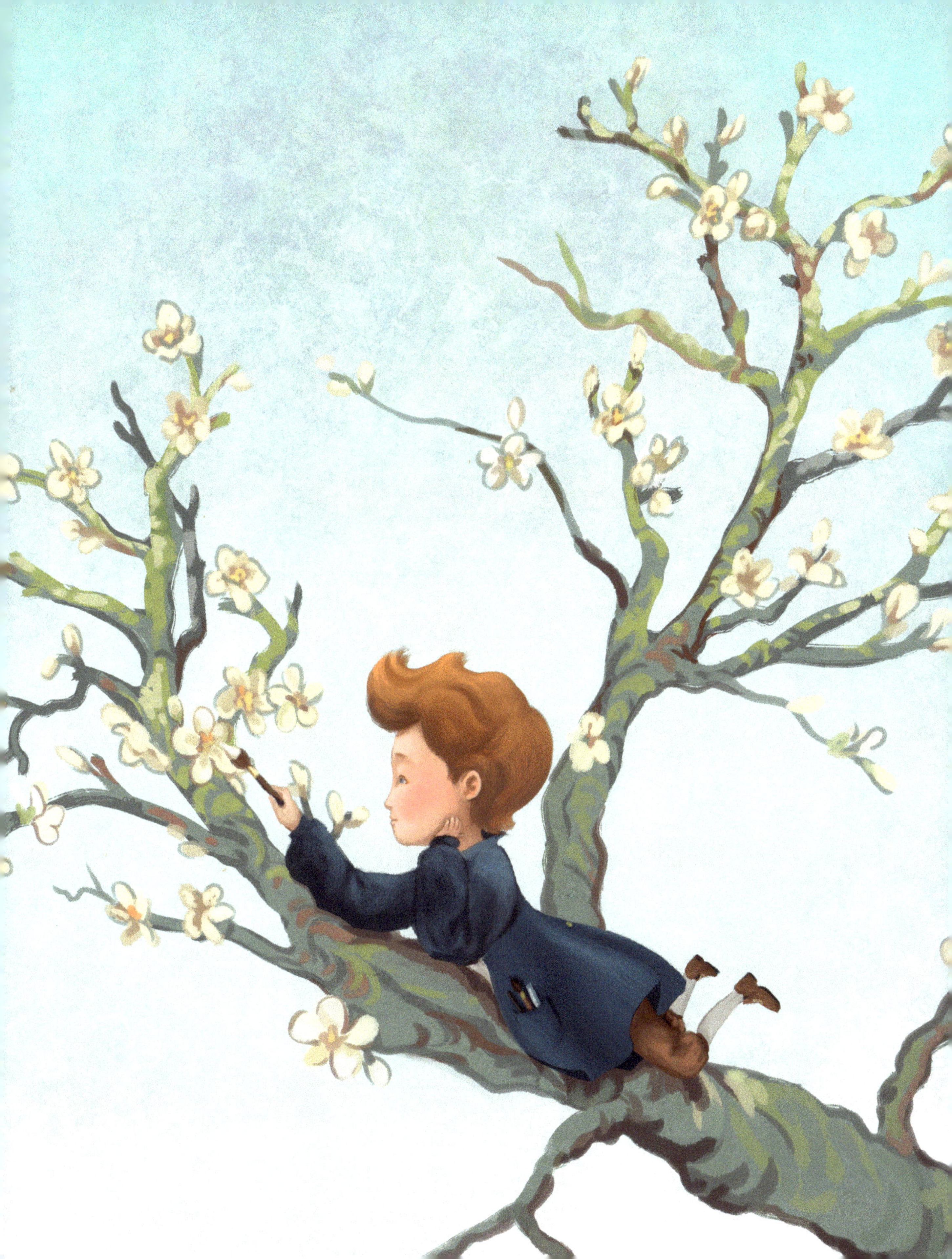

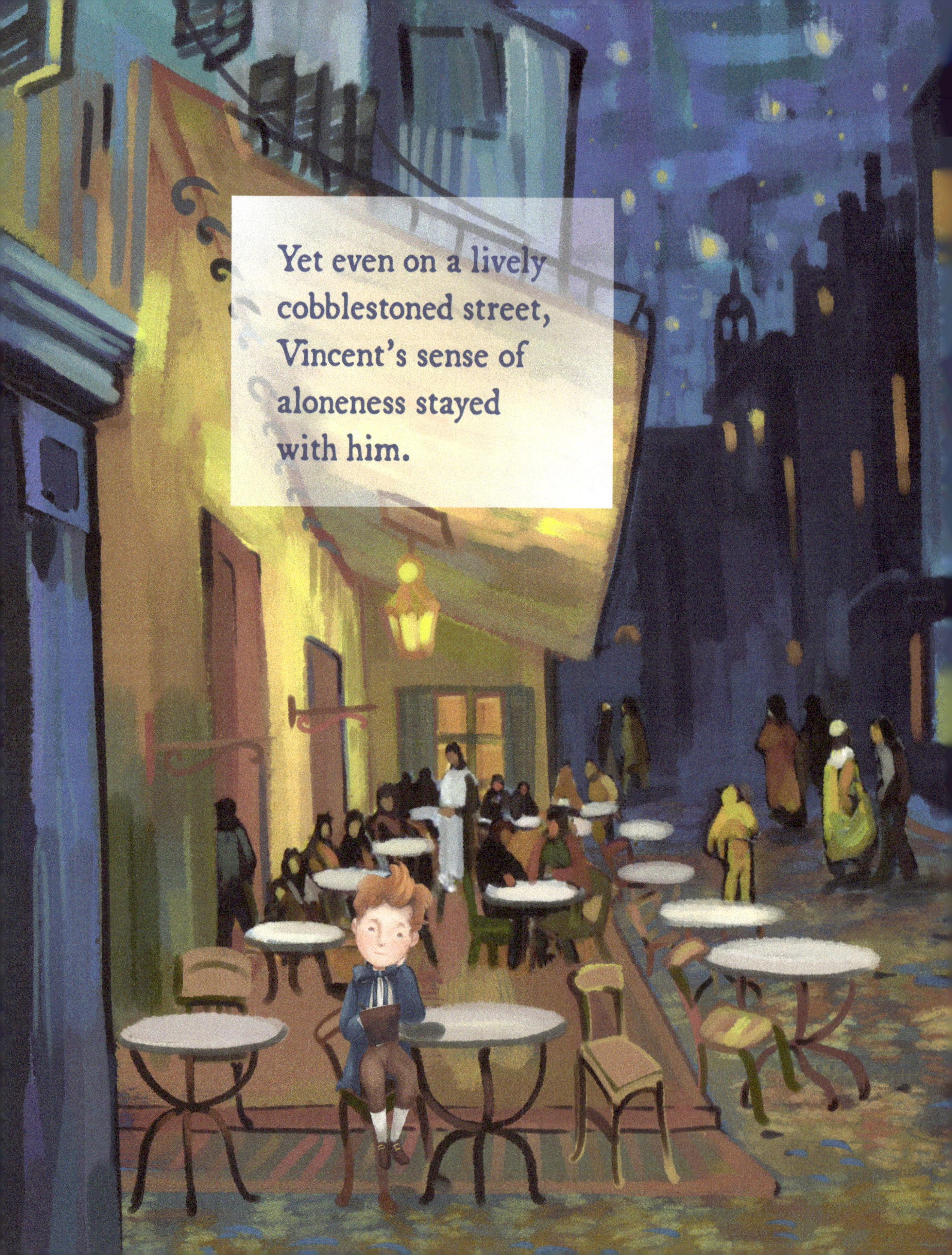
Yet even on a lively
cobblestoned street,
Vincent's sense of
aloneness stayed
with him.

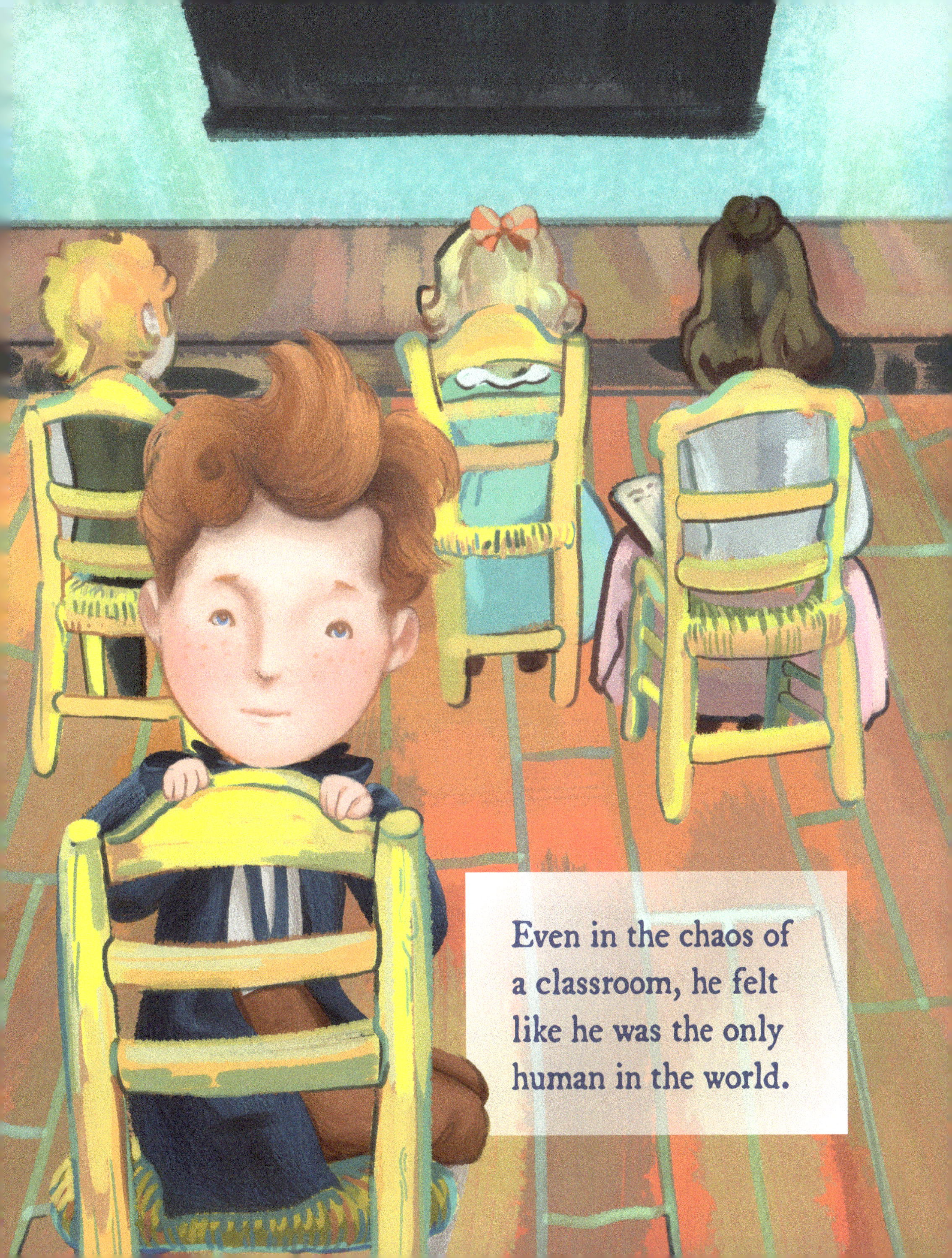
Even in the chaos of
a classroom, he felt
like he was the only
human in the world.

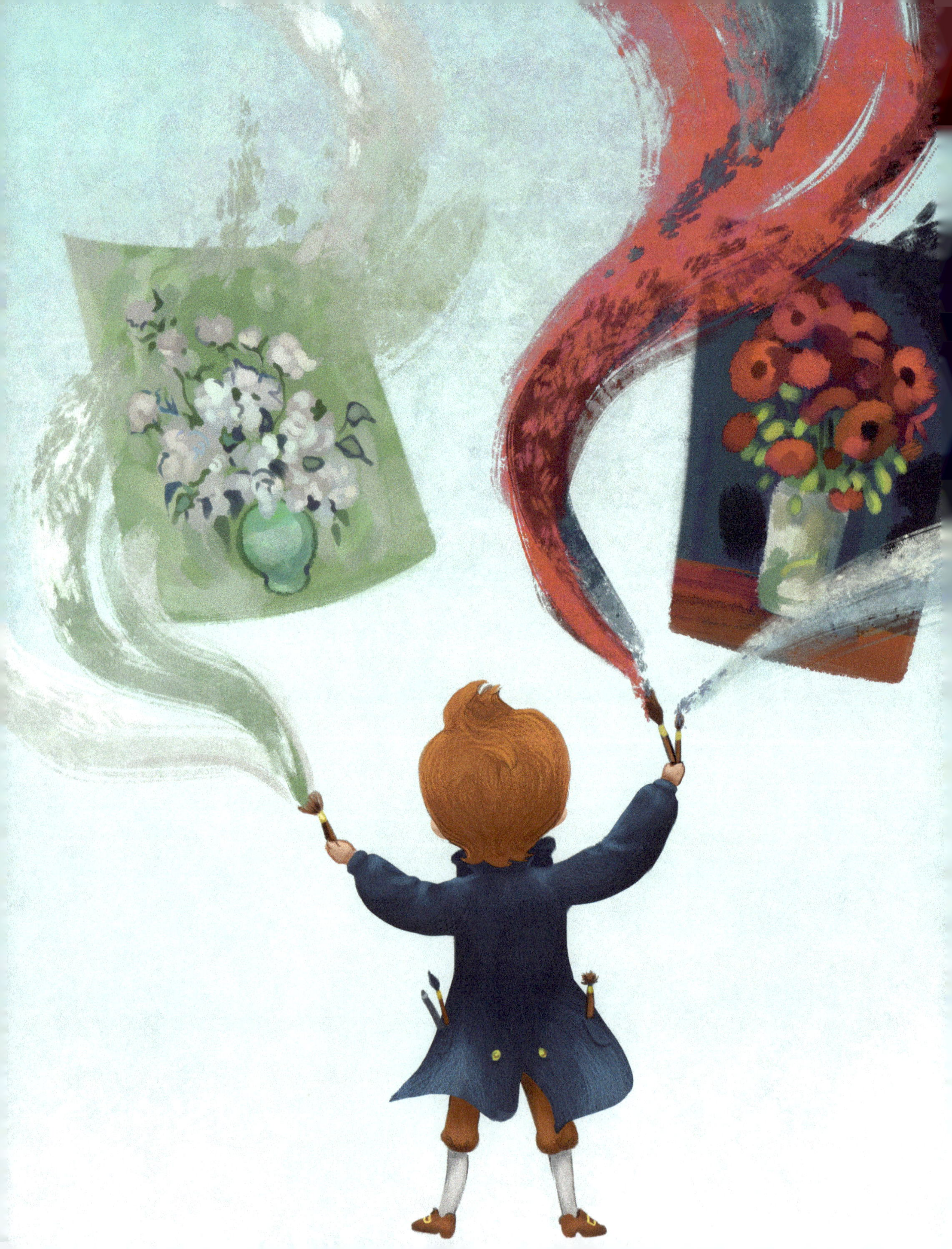

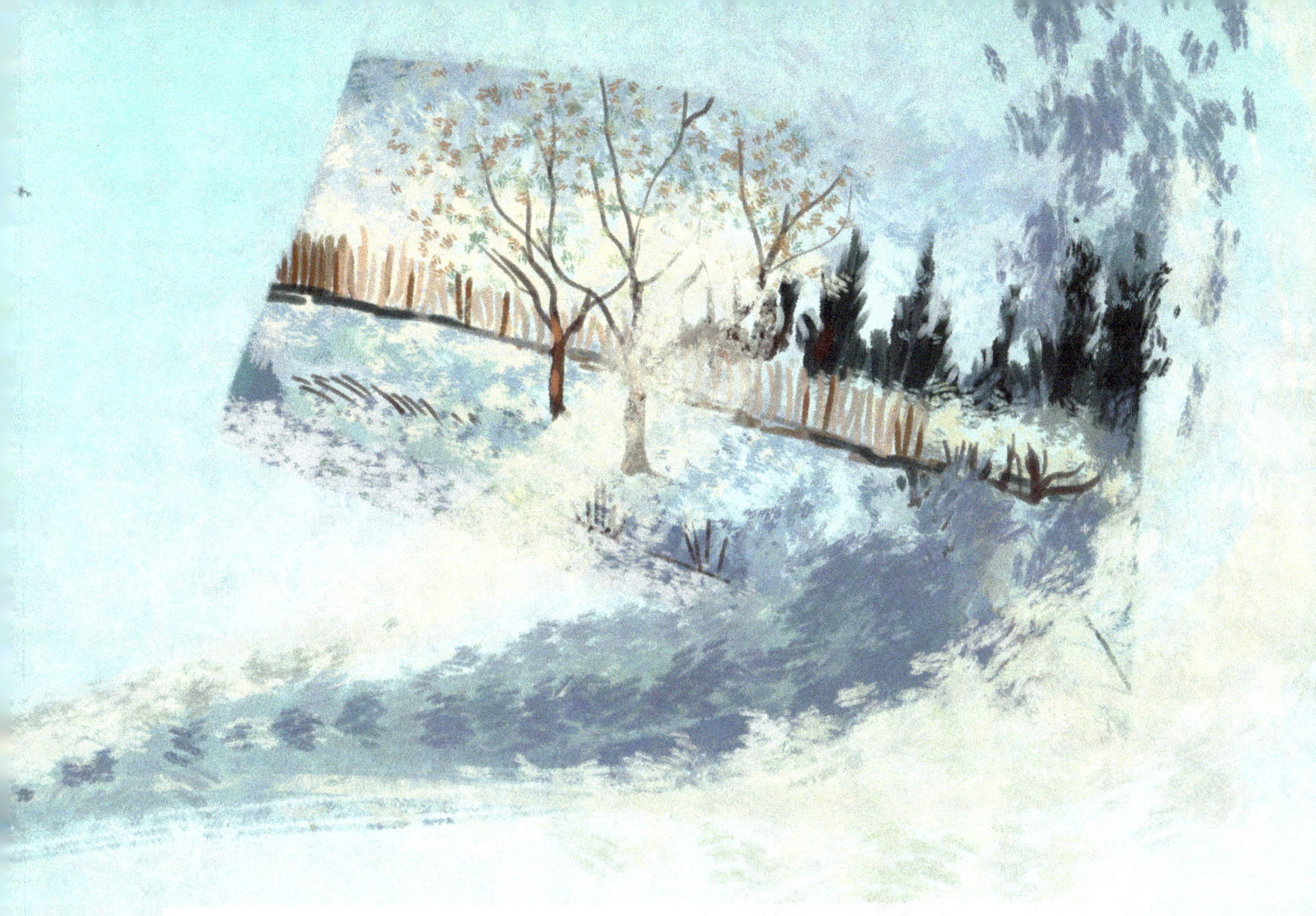

Still, his art reflected the stunning eyeful he saw in the world around him. But only if you knew where to look.

Like in the roses.

And in the poppies.

And in the stillest of winter days.

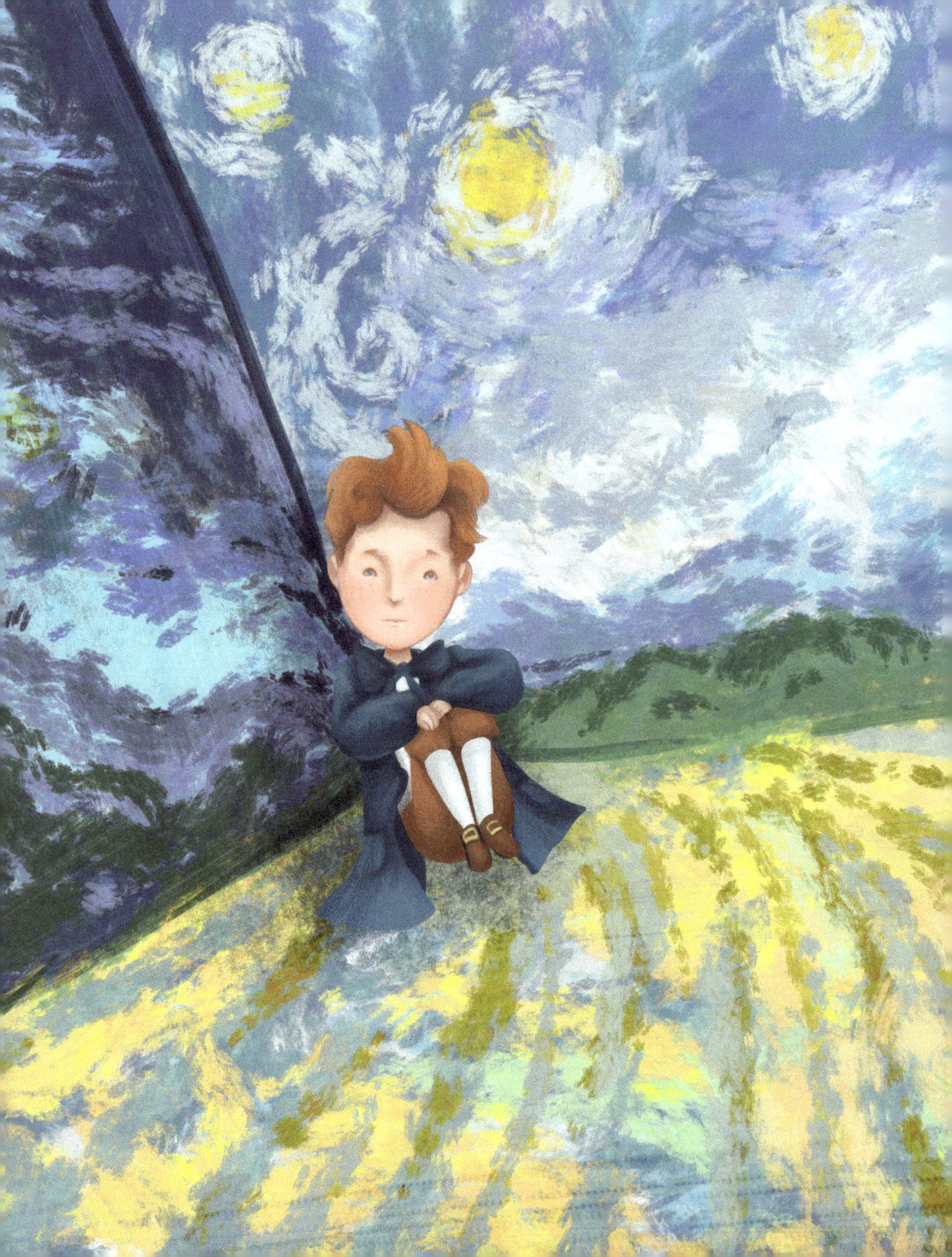

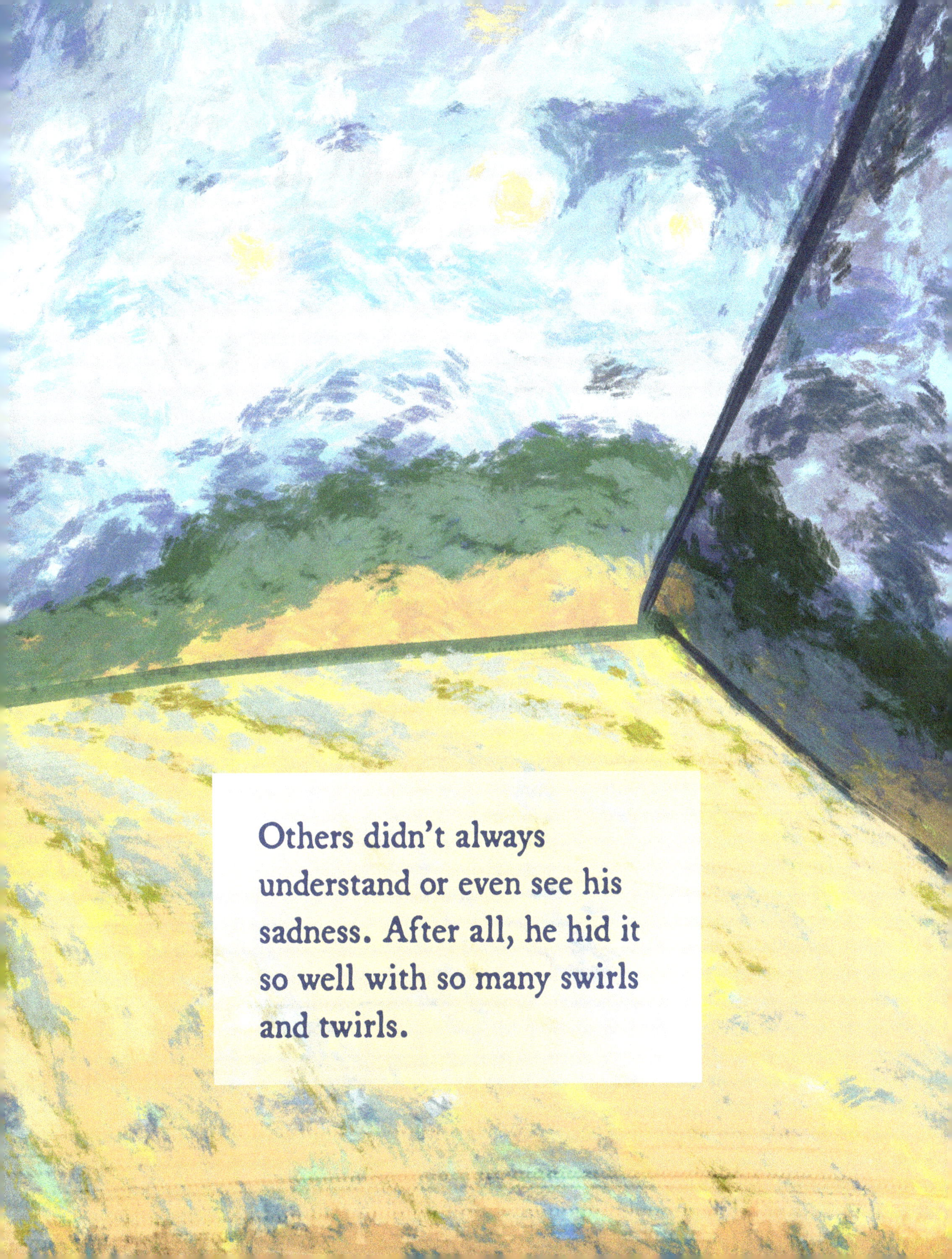

Others didn't always
understand or even see his
sadness. After all, he hid it
so well with so many swirls
and twirls.

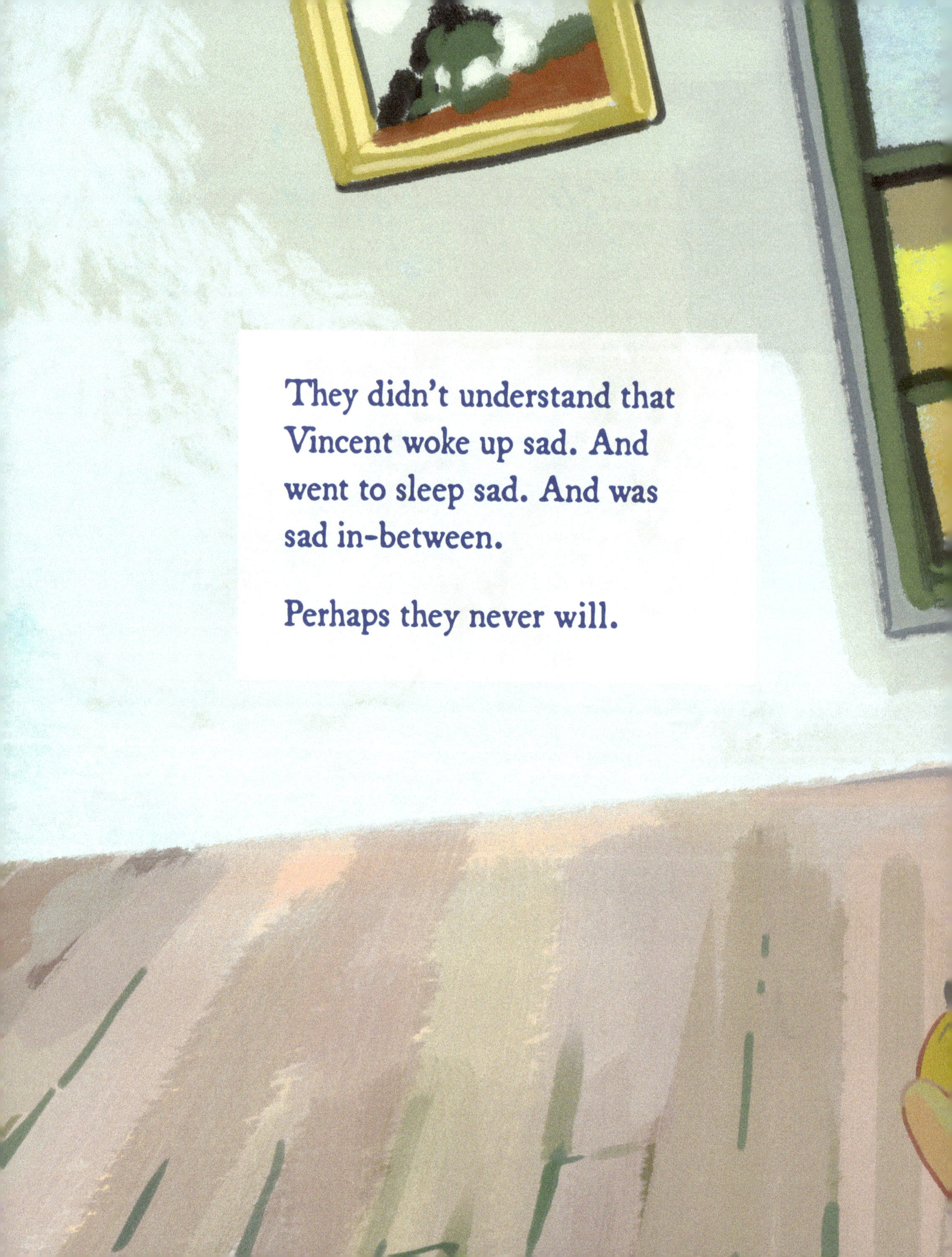

They didn't understand that
Vincent woke up sad. And
went to sleep sad. And was
sad in-between.

Perhaps they never will.

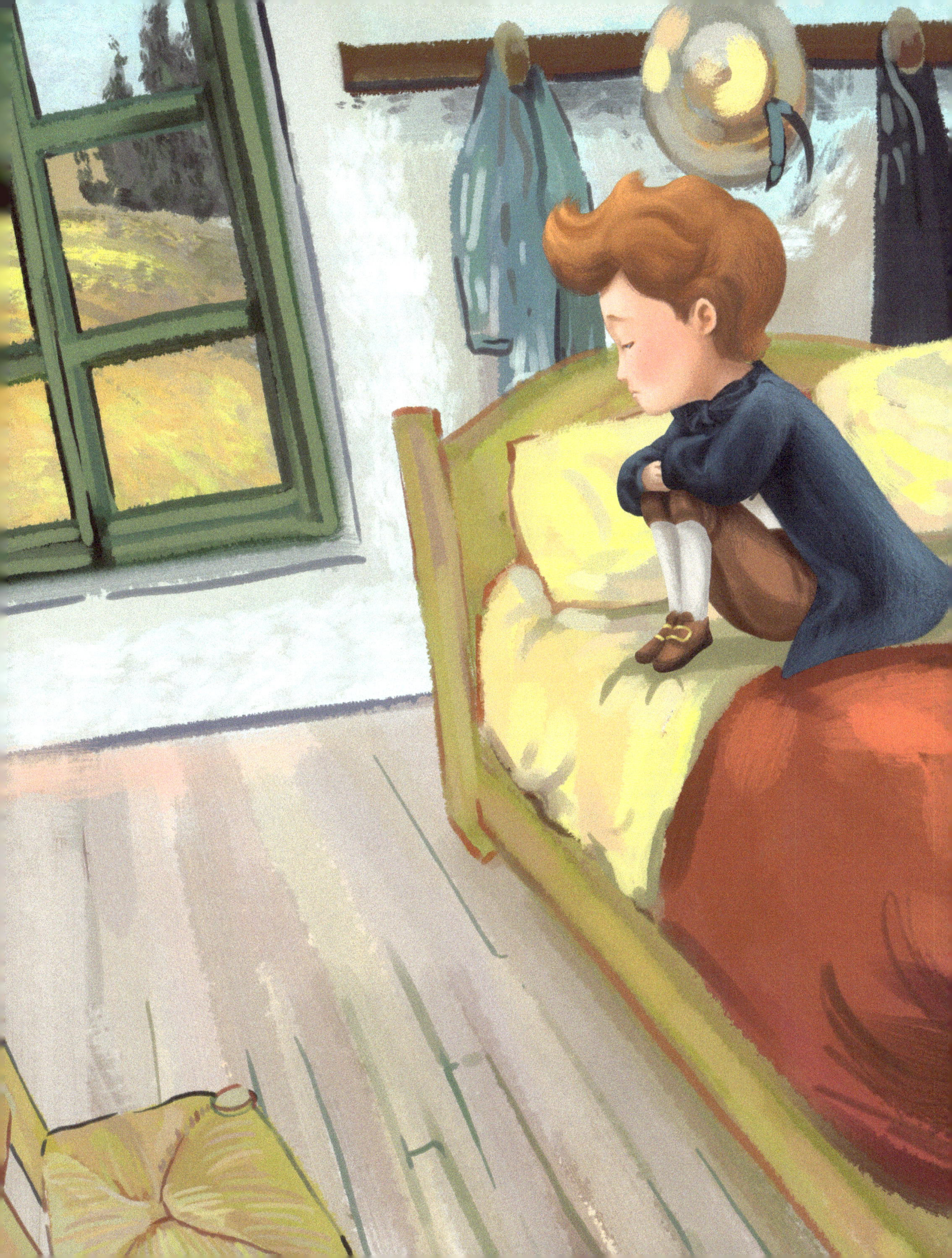

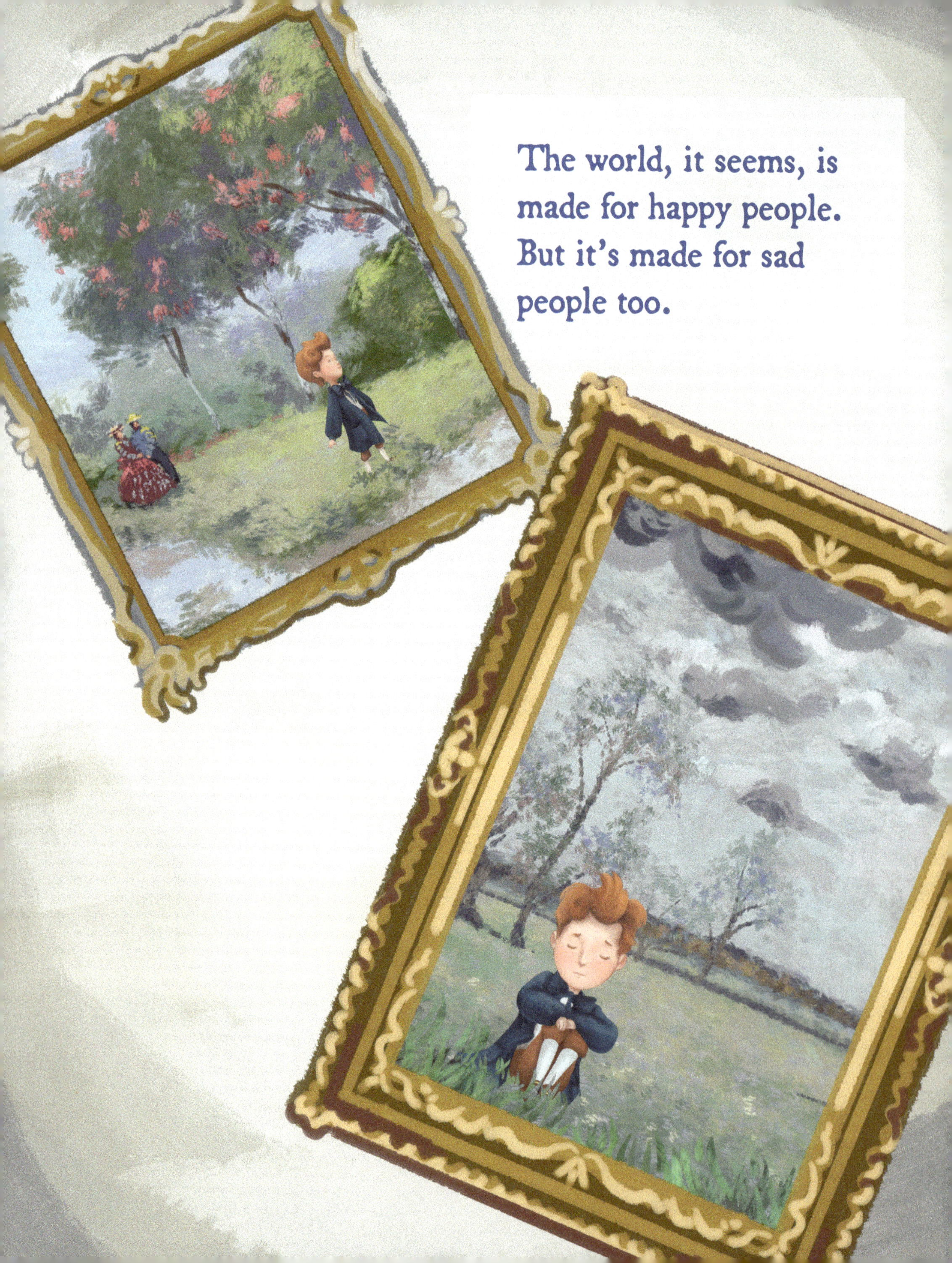

The world, it seems, is made for happy people. But it's made for sad people too.

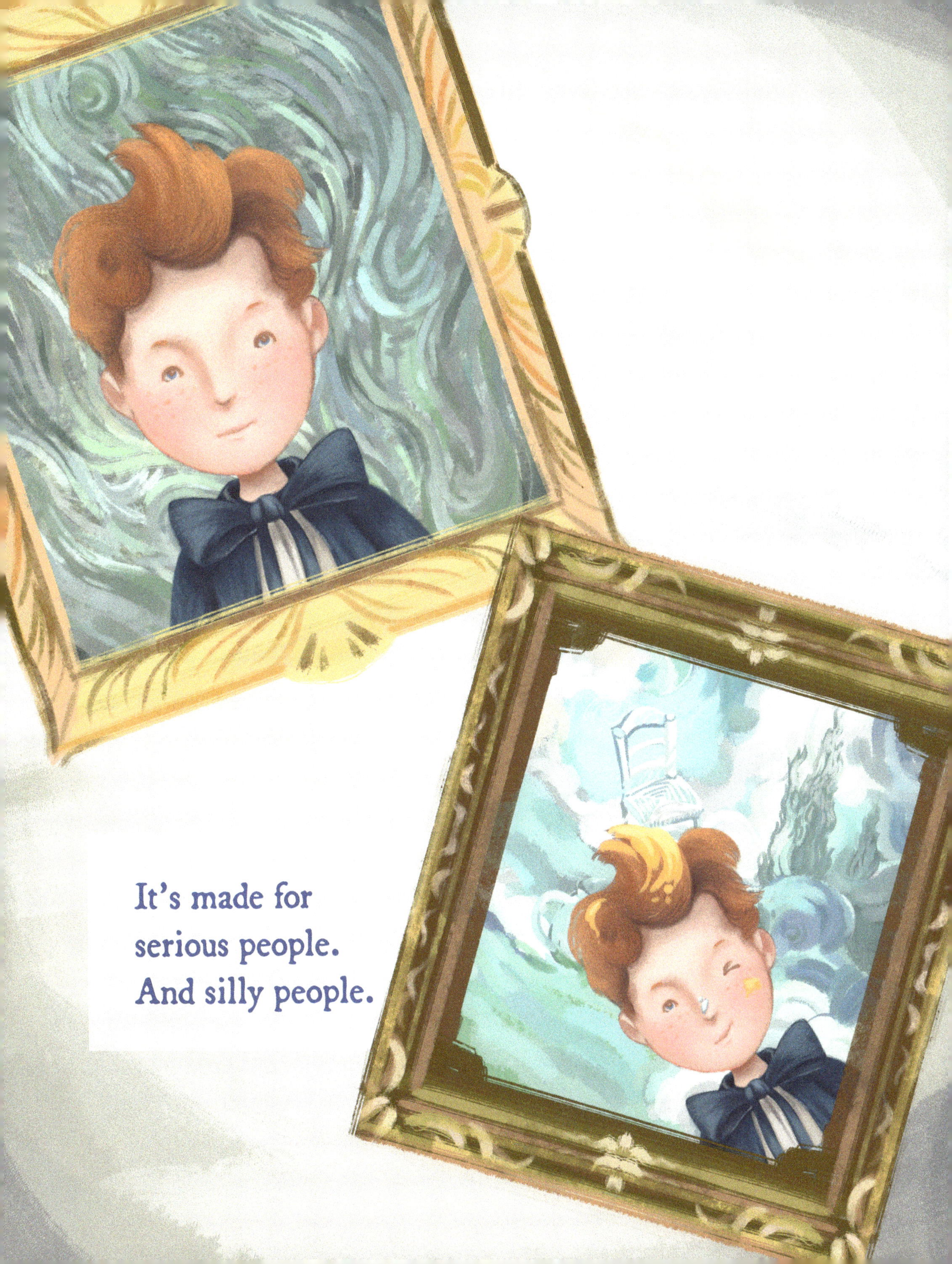

It's made for
serious people.
And silly people.

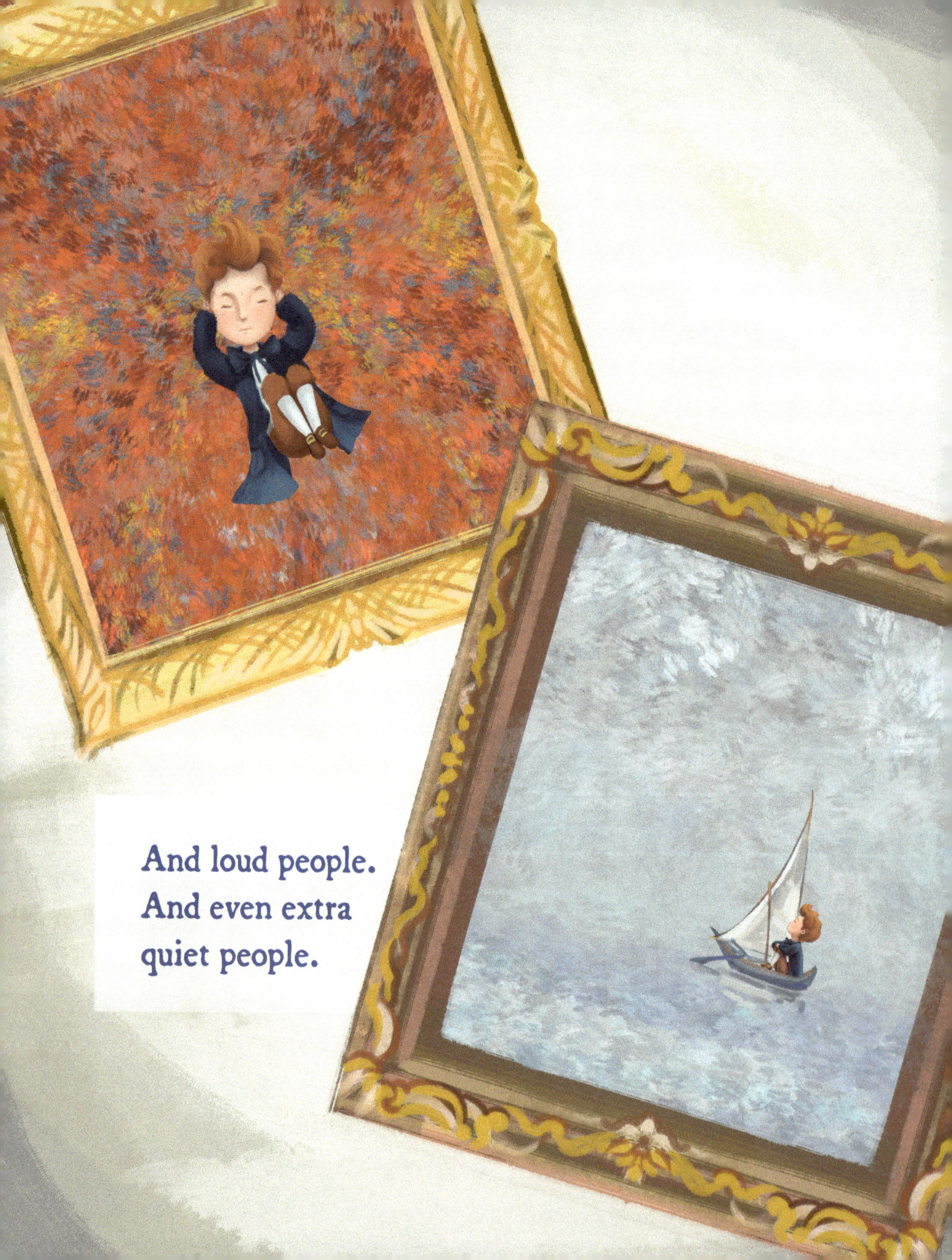

And loud people.
And even extra
quiet people.

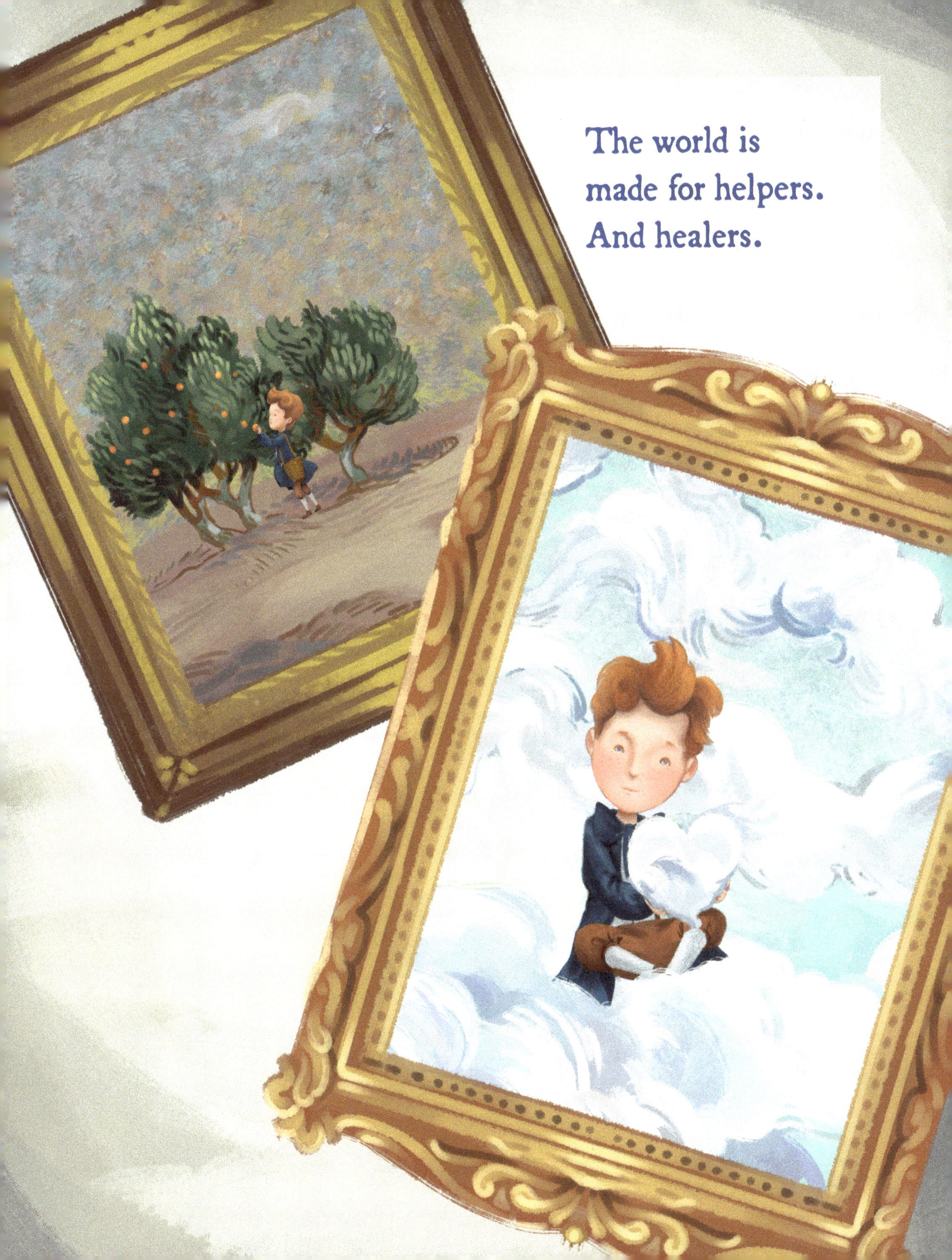

The world is
made for helpers.
And healers.

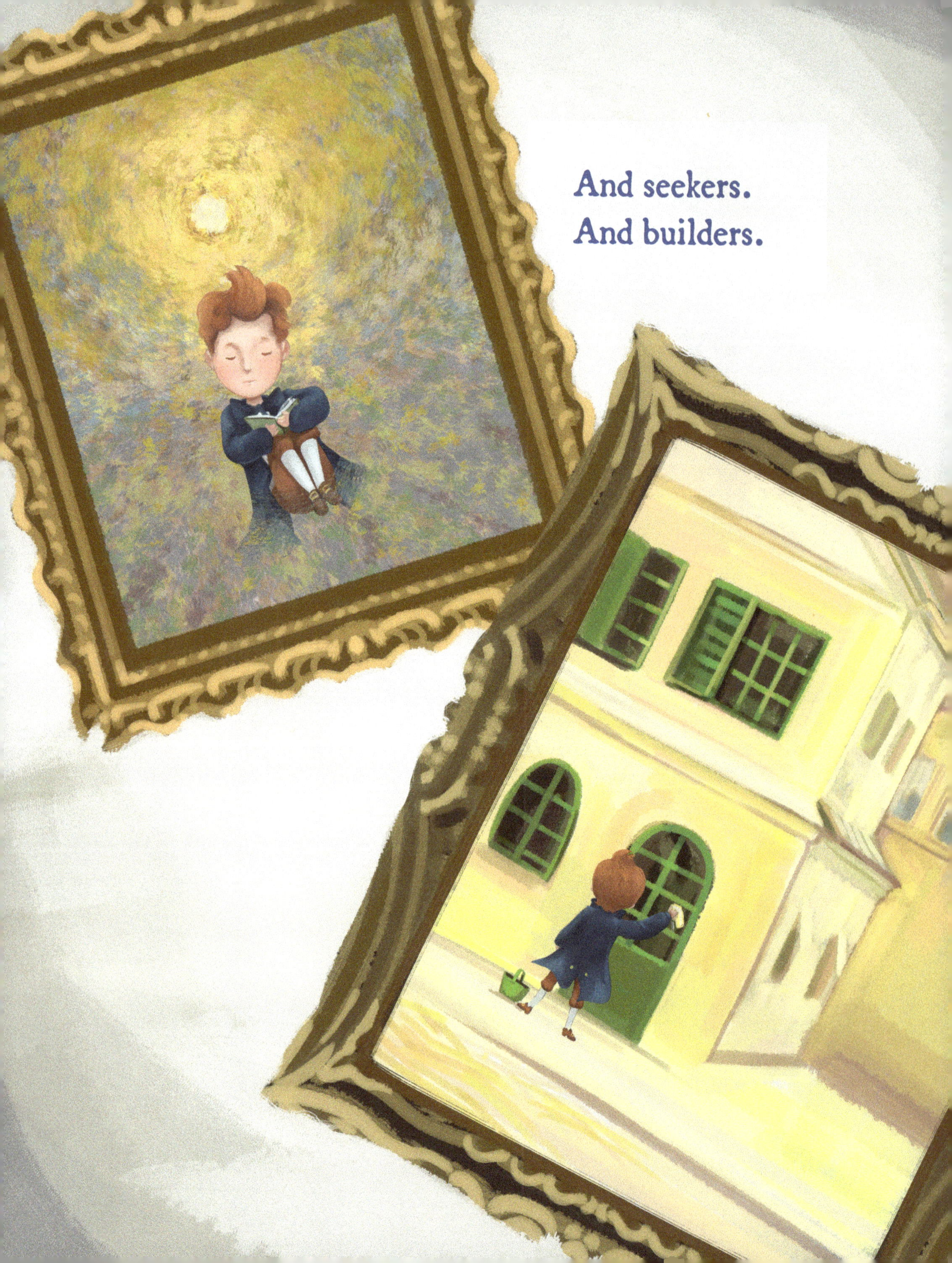

And seekers.
And builders.

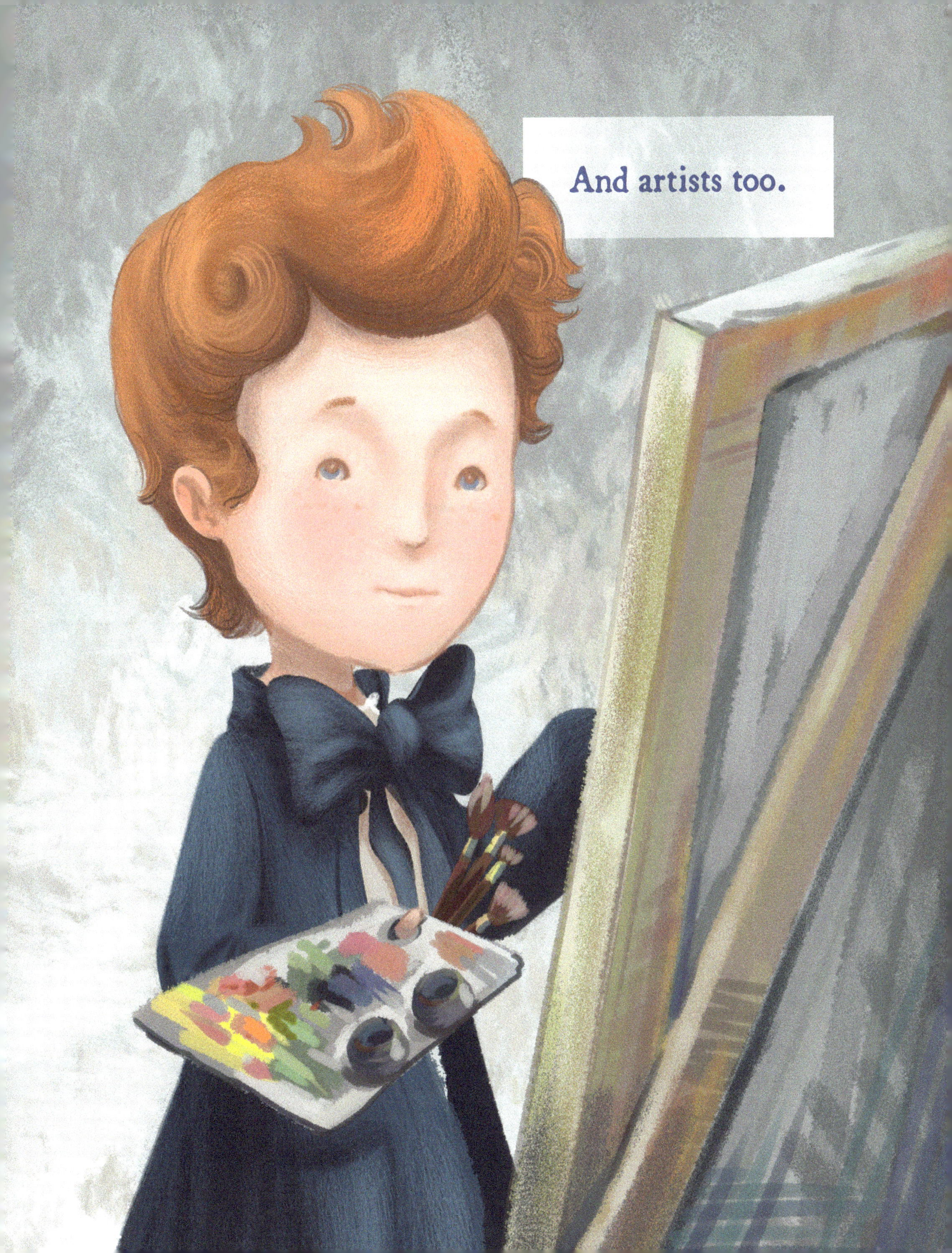
And artists too.

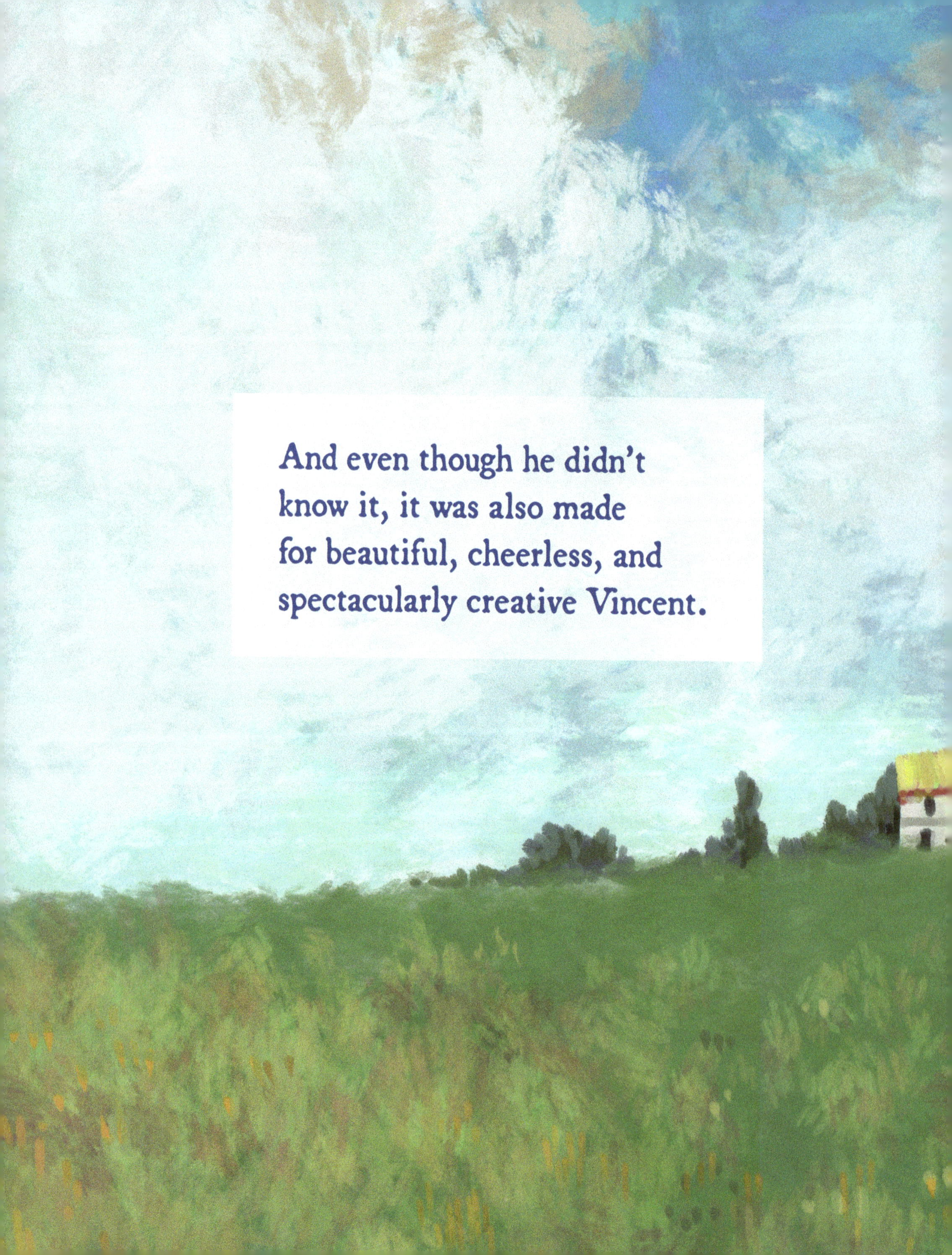

And even though he didn't
know it, it was also made
for beautiful, cheerless, and
spectacularly creative Vincent.

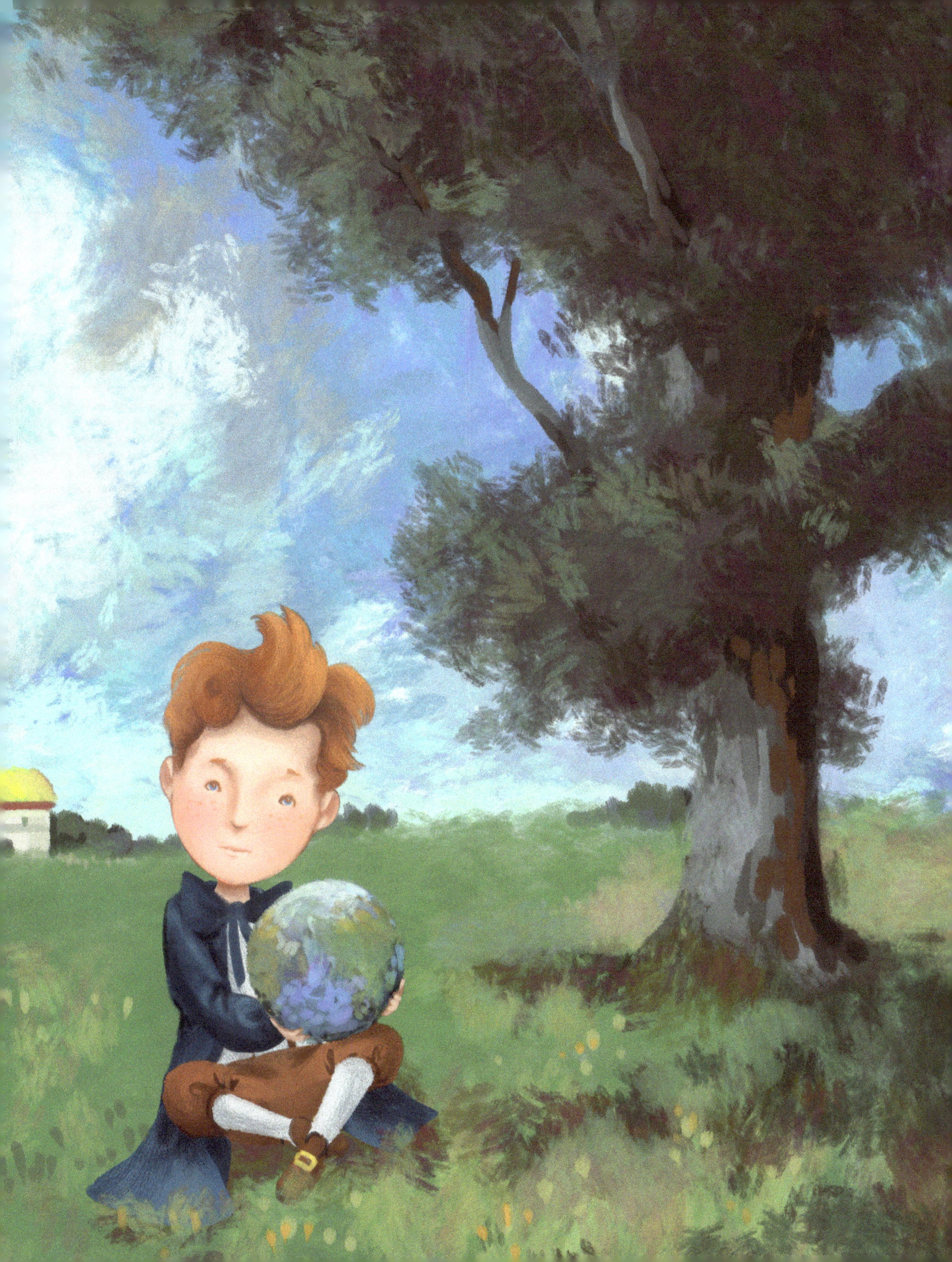

So on starry starry
nights and cold and
wintry days, Vincent
chased his blues and
grays, grabbing all of
the feelings with his
pens and pencils and
chalks and brushes.

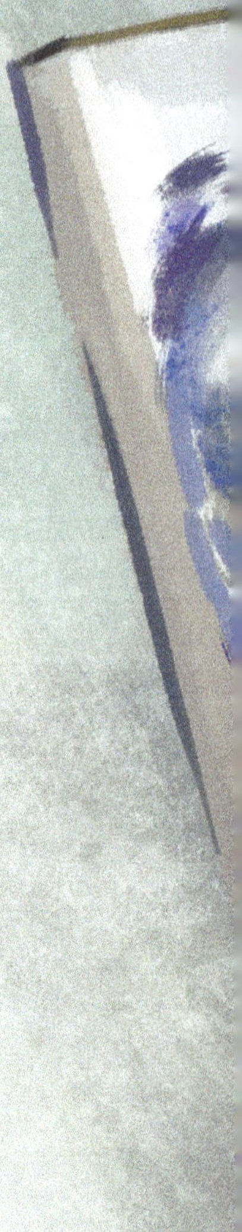

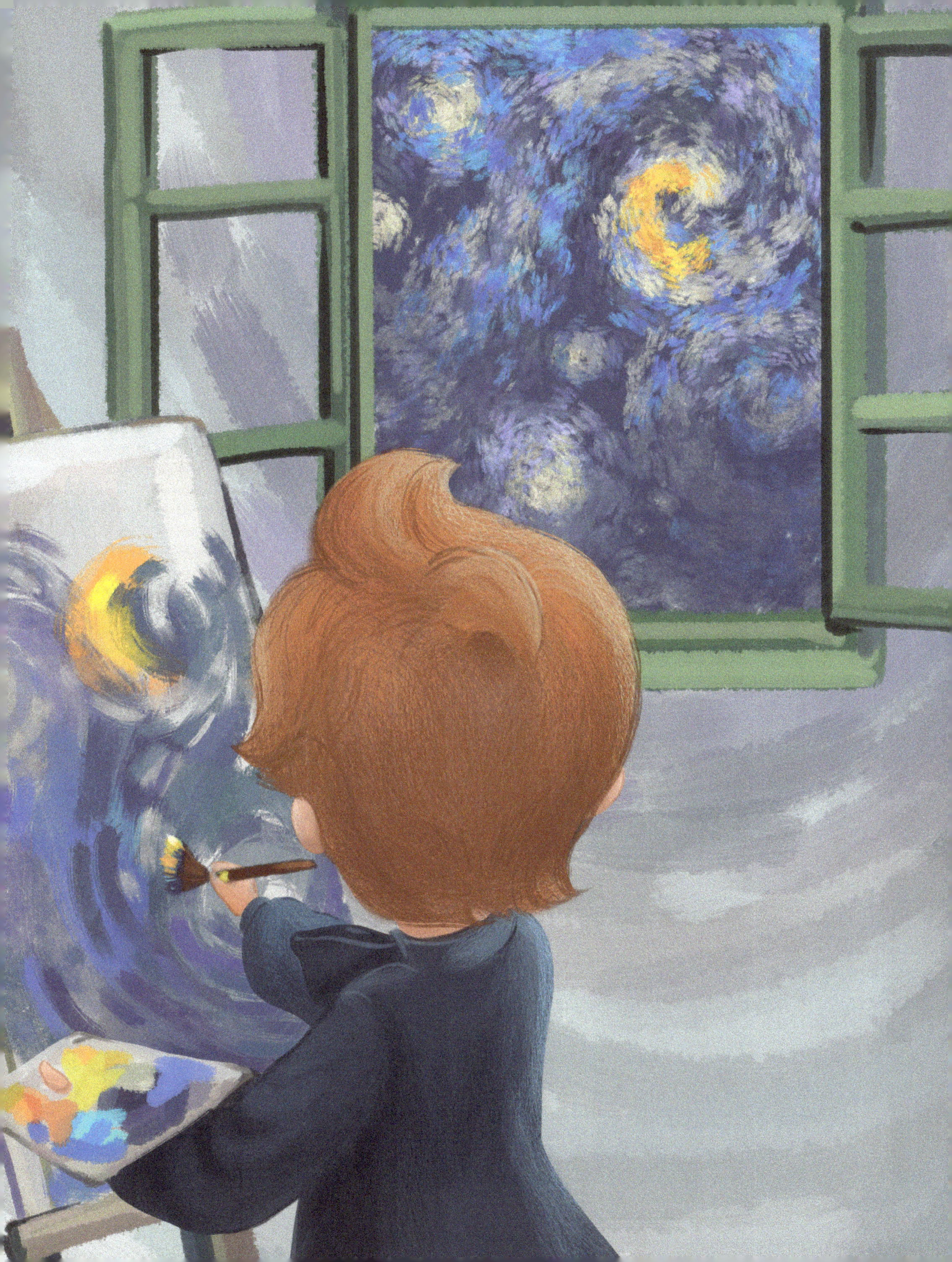

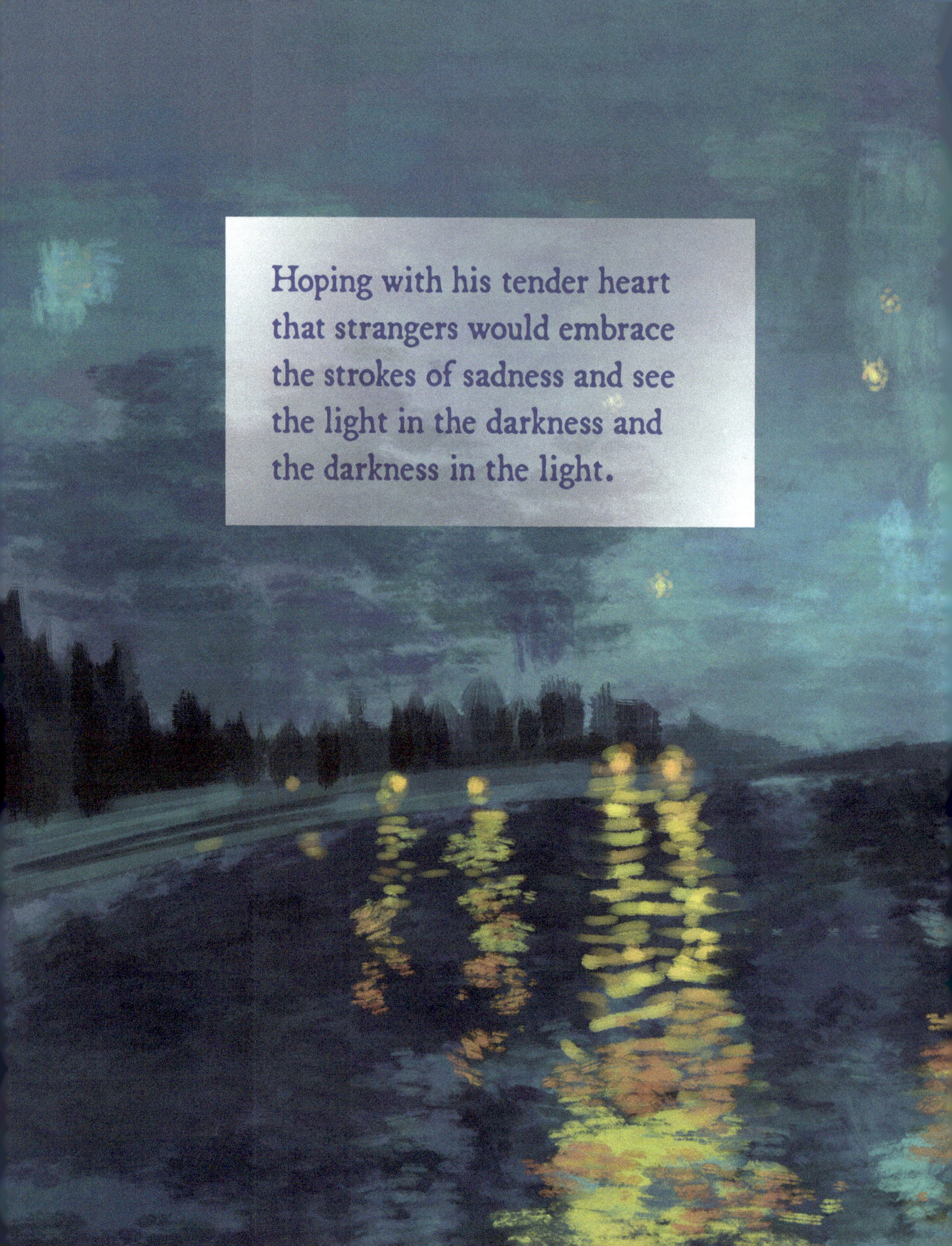

Hoping with his tender heart
that strangers would embrace
the strokes of sadness and see
the light in the darkness and
the darkness in the light.

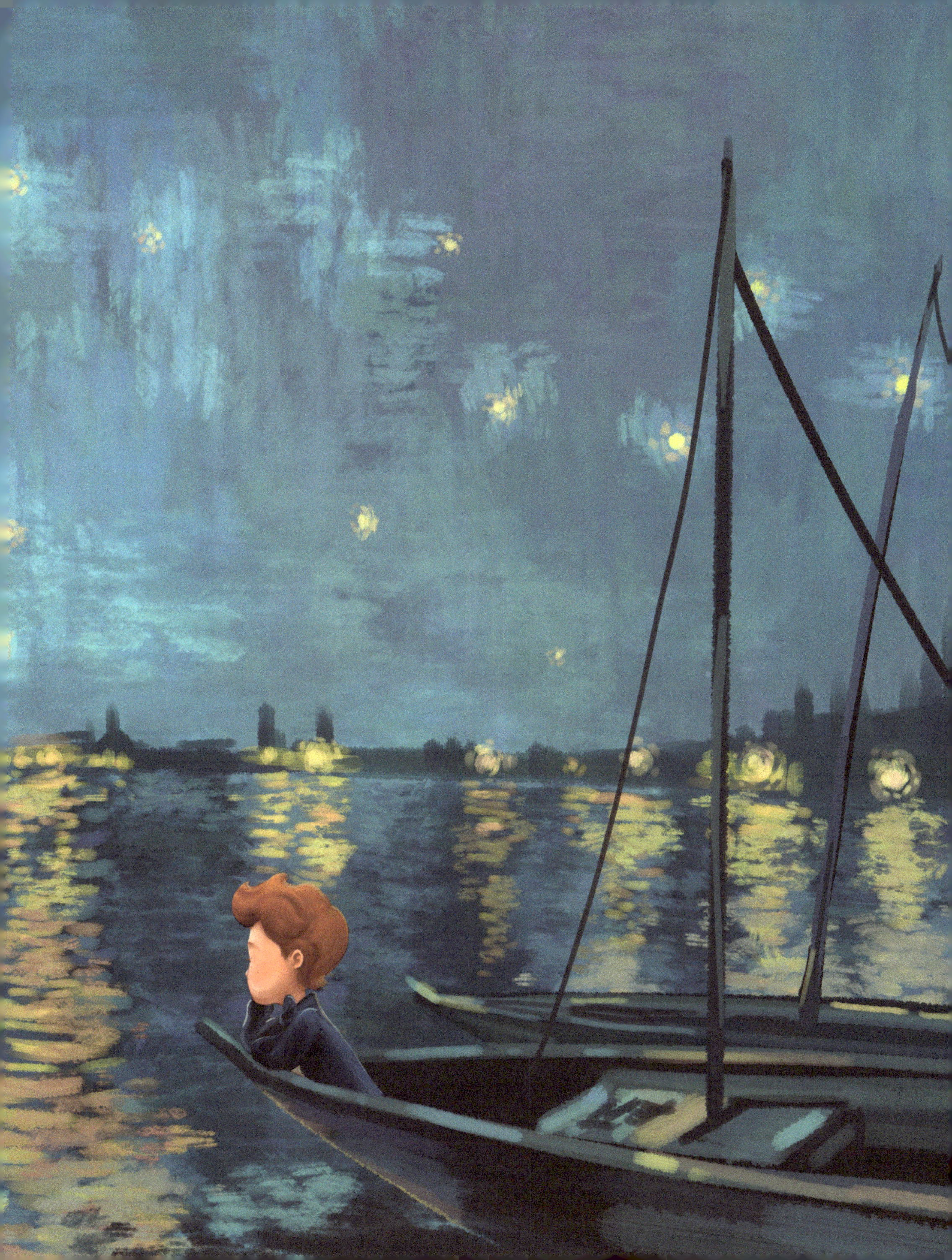

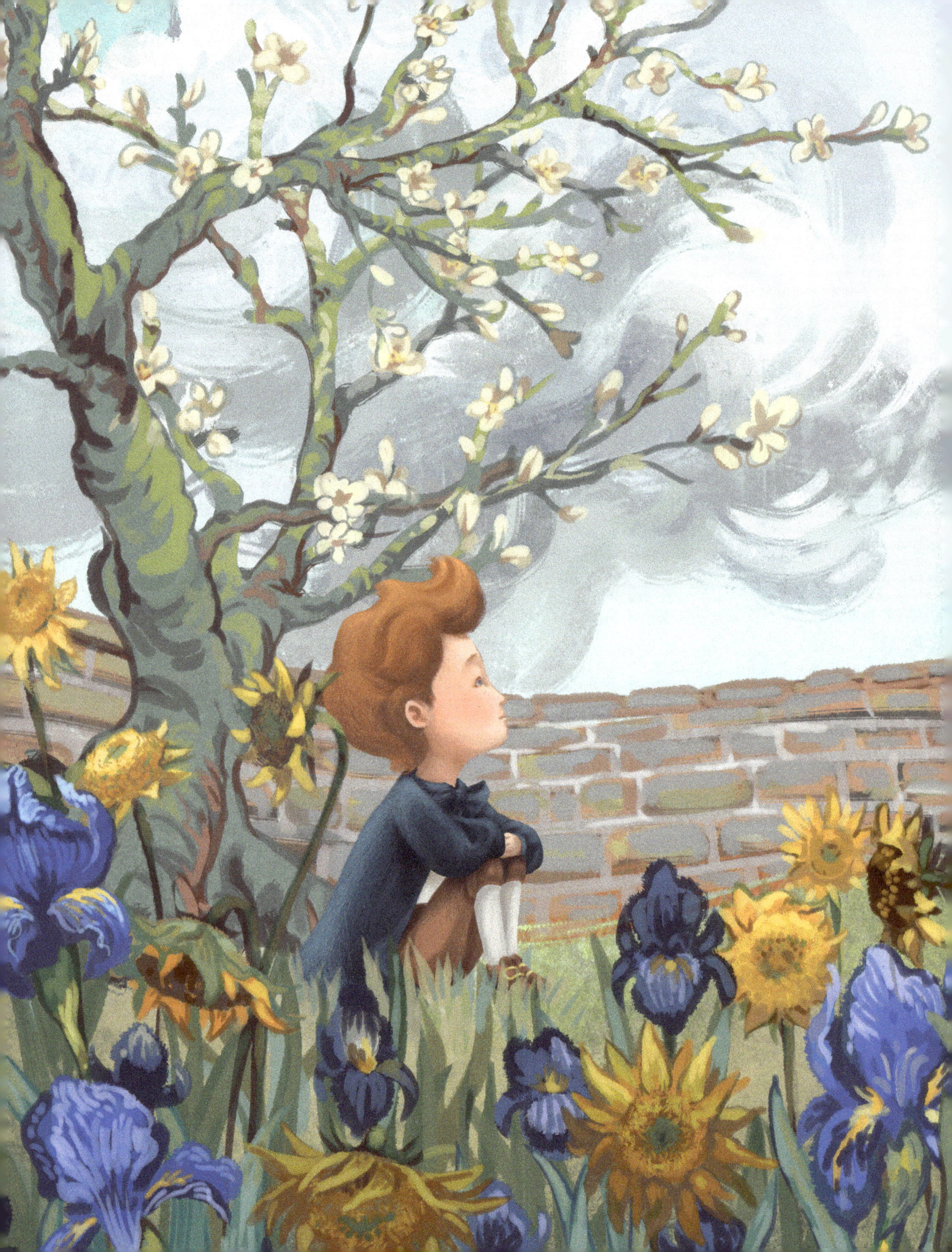

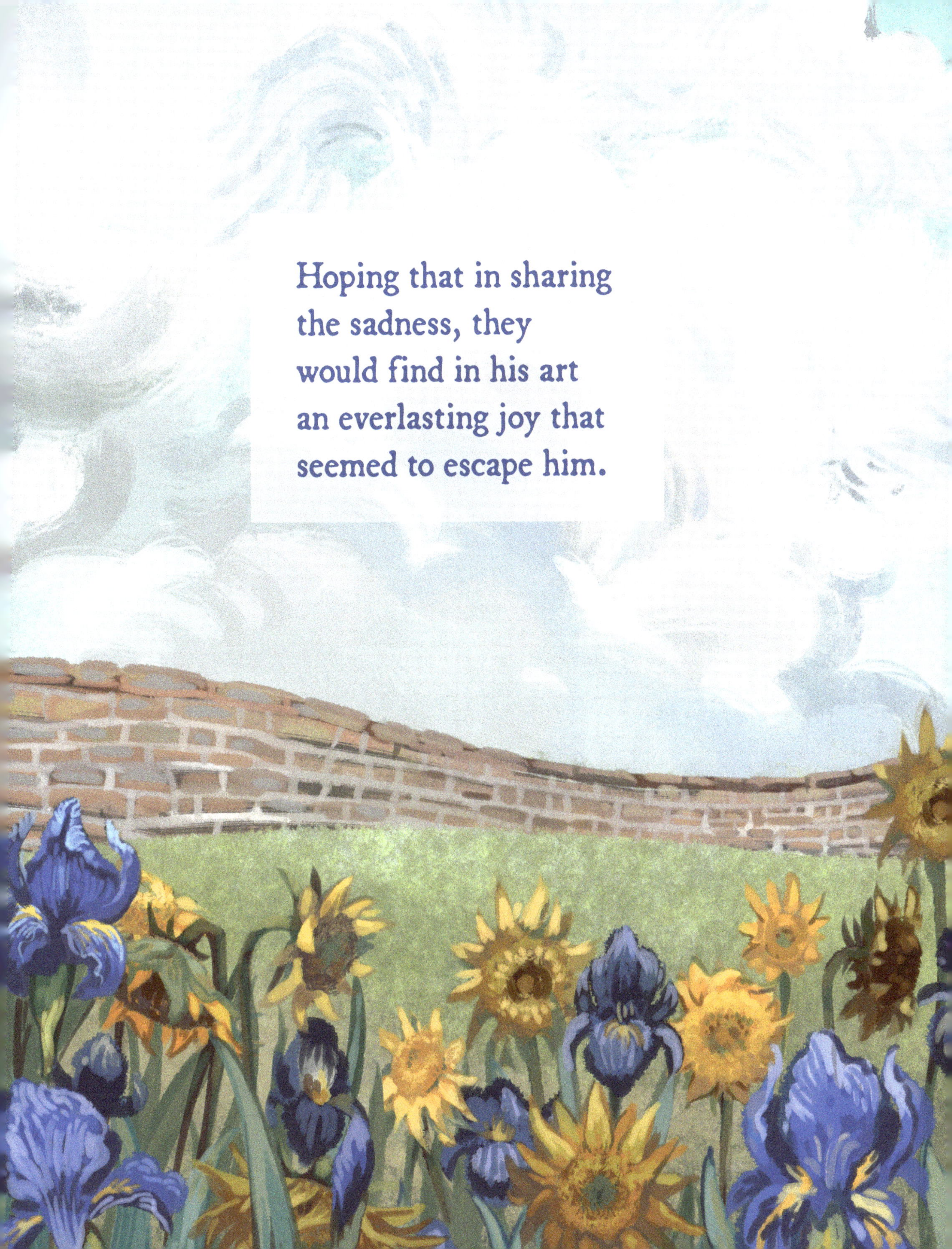
Hoping that in sharing
the sadness, they
would find in his art
an everlasting joy that
seemed to escape him.

Hoping that perhaps,
just perhaps, they'll
know where to look,
they'll see what he
felt...and that they'll
listen now.

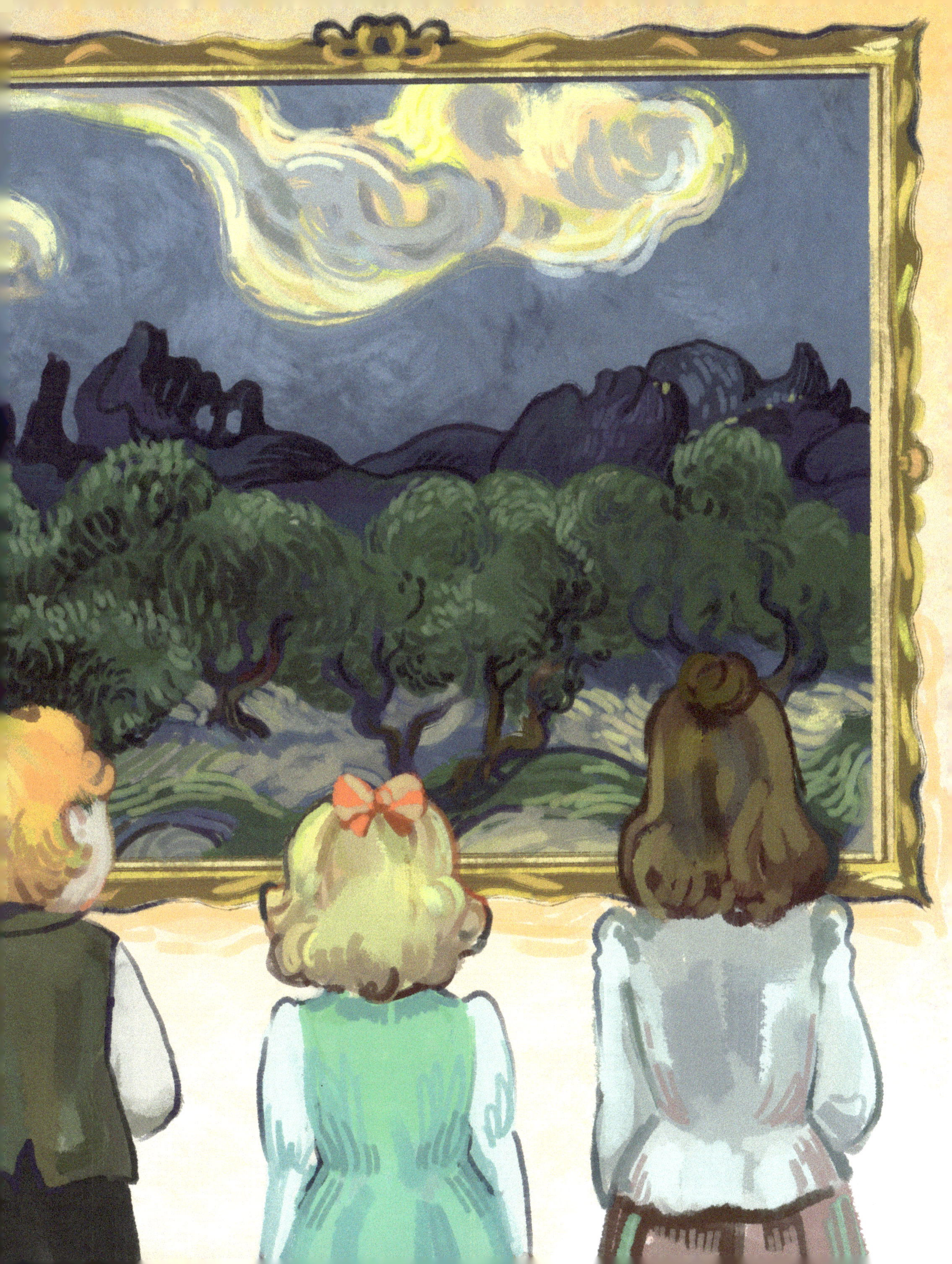

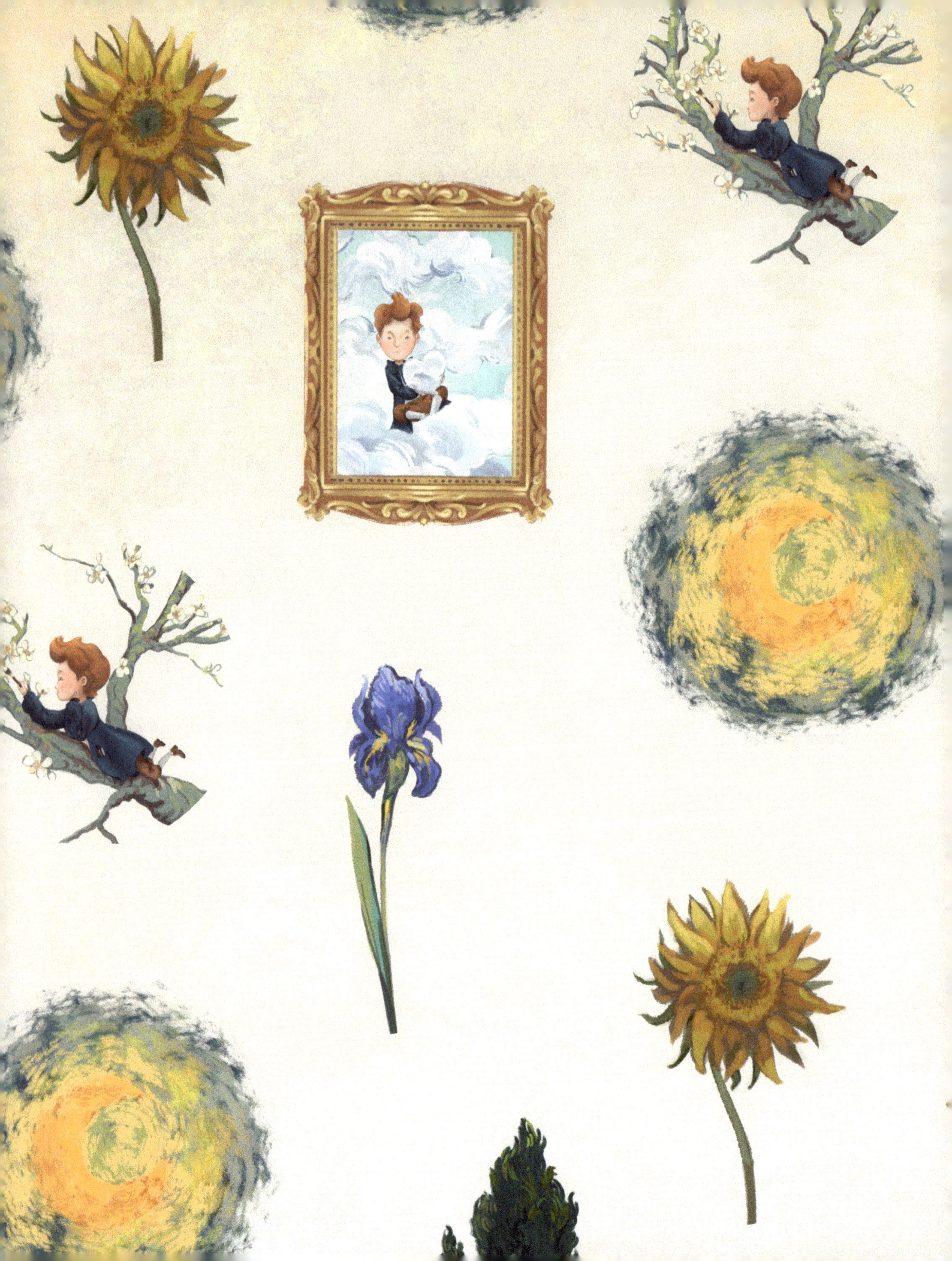

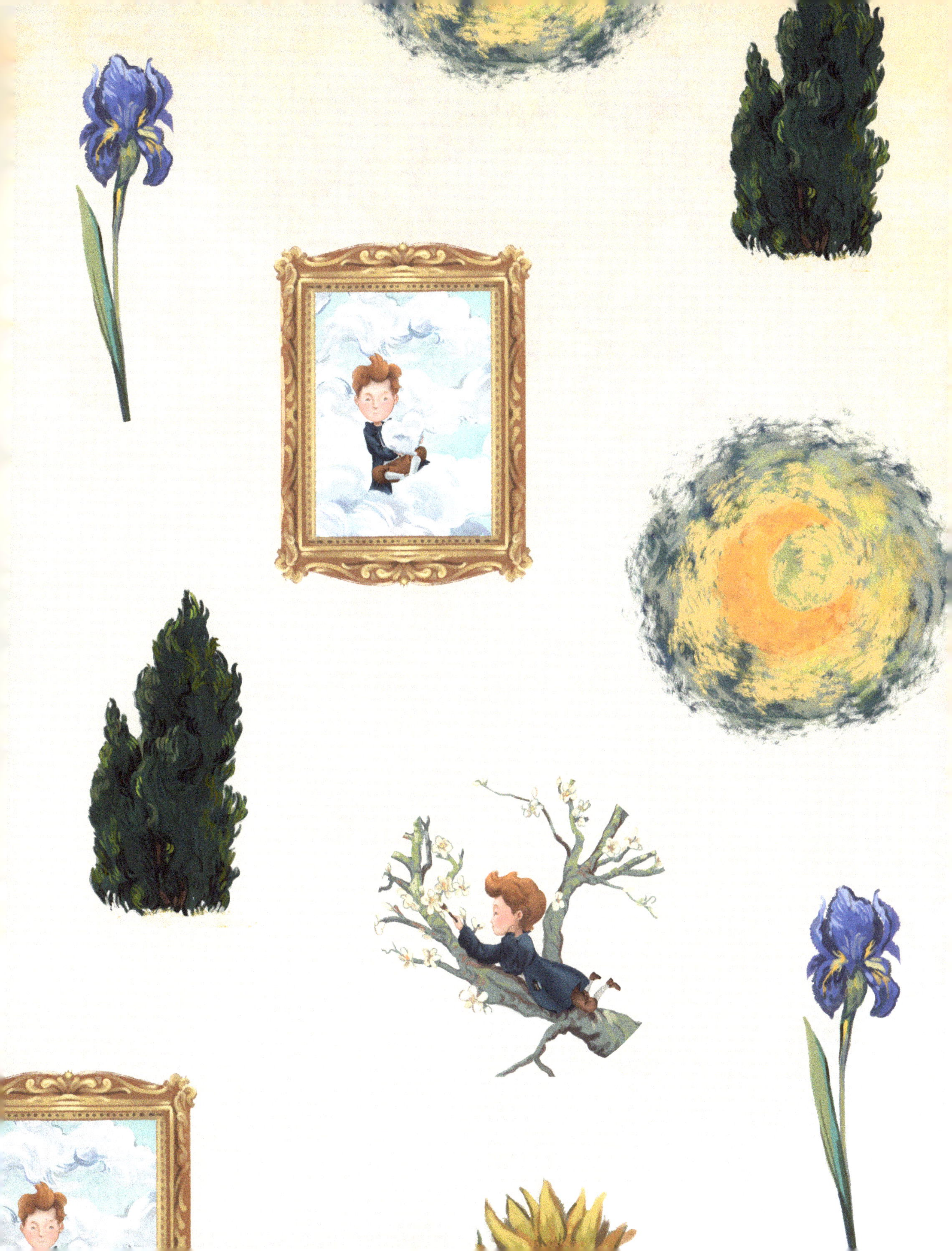